W9-ATF-493

Then Shall Your Light Rise

Then Shall Your Light Rise

Spiritual Formation
and
Social Witness

Joyce Hollyday

UPPER
ROOM BOOKS
NASHVILLE

THEN SHALL YOUR LIGHT RISE
SPIRITUAL FORMATION AND SOCIAL WITNESS
© 1997 by Joyce Hollyday
All rights reserved.

No part of this book may be used or reproduced in any manner whatsoever without permission except in the case of brief quotations embodied in critical articles or reviews. For information, write Upper Room Books, P.O. Box 189, Nashville, TN 37202-0189.

Scripture quotations not otherwise identified are from the New Revised Standard Version of the Bible, © 1989 by the Division of Christian Education of the National Council of the Churches of Christ in the USA. Used by permission. All rights reserved.

KJV designates quotations from the King James Version of the Bible.

Scripture quotations designated RSV are from the Revised Standard Version of the Bible, copyrighted 1846, 1952, and ©1971 by the Division of Christian Education, National Council of the Churches of Christ in the USA. Used by permission.

Chapter opening graphic reprinted from *Clip Art for the Liturgical Year CD-Rom*, The Liturgical Press, 1996. Used with permission of the copyright holder.

While every effort has been made to secure permission, we may have failed in a few cases to trace or contact the copyright holder. We apologize for any inadvertent oversight or error.

Cover Illustration: Kathleen Edwards
The Upper Room Web Site: http://www.upperroom.org
First printing: April 1997 (5)

Library of Congress Cataloging-in-Publication
Hollyday, Joyce.
      Then shall your light rise: spiritual formation and social witness / Joyce Hollyday.
            p.   cm.
      ISBN 0-8358-0816-5
      1. Spiritual formation. 2. Christian life.   I. Title.
BV4051.2.H5654   1997
248.4—dc21   97-8990
                                                                CIP
Printed in the United States of America on acid-free paper

or the earliest lights in my life:

my parents,
Ann and Robert Hollyday

my sisters,
Kay Filar and Debra Link

the church family at First United Methodist
on Chocolate Avenue in Hershey, Pennsylvania

and *Daniel Berrigan,*
who prays as passionately as he protests

Across the world, across the street,
The victims of injustice cry
For shelter and for bread to eat,
And never live until they die.

Then let the servant church arise,
A caring church that longs to be
A partner in Christ's sacrifice,
And clothed in Christ's humanity.
✤ Fred Pratt Green

Taken from "The Church of Christ in Every Age" by Fred Pratt
Green © 1971 by Hope Publishing Co., Carol Stream, IL 60188.
All rights reserved. Used by permission.

Contents

Introduction

IS NOT THIS THE FAST THAT I CHOOSE:
    to loose the bonds of injustice,
    to undo the thongs of the yoke,
to let the oppressed go free,
    and to break every yoke?
Is it not to share your bread with the hungry,
    and bring the homeless poor into your house;
when you see the naked, to cover them,
    and not to hide yourself from your own kin?
Then your light shall break forth like the dawn,
    and your healing shall spring up quickly;
your vindicator shall go before you,
    the glory of the Lord shall be your rear guard.
Then you shall call, and the Lord will answer;
you shall cry for help, and [God] will say,
    Here I am.

If you remove the yoke from among you,
    the pointing of the finger,
        the speaking of evil,
if you pour yourself out for the hungry
    and satisfy the needs of the afflicted,
then shall your light rise in the darkness
    and your gloom be like the noonday.

The Lord will guide you continually,
 and satisfy your needs in parched places,
 and make your bones strong;
and you shall be like a watered garden,
 like a spring of water,
  whose waters never fail.
Your ancient ruins shall be rebuilt;
 you shall raise up the foundations
  of many generations;
you shall be called the repairer of the breach,
 the restorer of streets to live in.
    → Isaiah 58:6-12; vv. 10a, 10c, RSV

WHAT IMAGES COME TO MIND WHEN you hear the phrase *spiritual discipline*? Some will think of daily prayer or Bible reading. Others may consider periods of fasting. Perhaps for some, the idea of spiritual discipline conjures up visions of cloistered monks who recite psalms and prayers throughout the day—a concept far removed from the daily demands of late twentieth-century life in North America.

For the ancient Hebrews, our ancestors in the faith, spiritual discipline and ritual were critical. Prayer, fasting, and instruction in holy living were the bedrock of faith formation. These avenues of devotion served as reminders that God was continually claiming the people as God's own. Together they shaped a memory that enabled faith to flourish through good times and bad, in exile and exaltation, through persecution and prosperity, in wilderness and promised land.

Today we have to work harder at finding rhythms and rituals of spirituality. Many of us live in urban and suburban settings quite removed from the seasons of sowing and harvest, productivity and rest, famine and abundance that shaped our ancestors' petitions and celebrations. Family schedules are fragmented, individual lives too busy. As a society, we spend many more hours watching television than praying, far more time being entertained than telling the stories of our faith. Secular rituals involving candy, toys, and painted eggs—all propelled by materialism—mark our holiest days. Perhaps most troubling of all, the growing societal breach between those of us who are comfortable and those who are barely surviving has undermined our sense of community.

Several years ago during Advent, the chaplain at Gettysburg College in Pennsylvania invited me to preach. After the service, I went to eat at her home and met her five-year-old son, Kyle.

Kyle's great accomplishment that season was his memorization of the Christmas story from the Bible. Both he and his mother were anxious to have him recite it. He started out strong and did well until he came to his favorite part, where the angels appeared to the shepherds and said, "Glory to God in the highest, and on earth, peace." He remembered the "Glory to God" part, but then his mind went blank.

His mother offered him some words of encouragement, and Kyle thought hard. Suddenly his face brightened, and he proudly launched into the story again: "And the angels appeared to the shepherds and said, 'Glory to God in the highest…and I'll huff and I'll puff and I'll blow your house down.'"

Without knowing it, my young friend Kyle offered an insightful commentary on the world. God's intention is for peace on earth, but there is a great deal of huffing and puffing.

AFTER MY TIME IN GETTYSBURG, I returned to my home in inner-city Washington, D.C., where I lived for fifteen years with Sojourners, an intentional Christian community. As I drove down my block that Christmas season, I saw piles of furniture and belongings dumped by the curb—the scant possessions of some of my neighbors who were being put out on the streets. Wealthy real-estate speculators were buying up the neighborhood in the name of urban renewal. The overnight shelters were packed that year, filled for the first time with mothers and children as well as single men.

Stories and images of homelessness and hunger, of dangerous urban war zones and destitute rural hollows, come our way all the time if our ears and eyes are open. Sometimes it seems easier not to listen or watch. But perhaps the more common response of caring Christians is a sense of feeling overwhelmed and paralyzed by the enormity of the suffering.

More and more, as I travel and listen, I hear materially comfortable Americans articulating a deep longing for spiritual roots and rhythms, for rituals that will infuse their lives with new meaning and bring them closer to God. At the same time, I hear the desperate pleas of those who cry to us from the streets and the soup kitchens, from the shacks and the shelters, for compassion and justice. These are not unrelated pleadings. They are in fact two sides of the same problem—and of the same hope. At heart, the crisis that divides our nation is a spiritual one. And only spiritual transformation will make us whole again.

The ancient Hebrews needed to be reminded of the connection between the material and spiritual, as do we. Their concern centered around offering the appropriate sacrifices and observing the proper fasts. But God, through the voice of the prophet Isaiah, redefined fasting for them. The sacrifice acceptable to God involves these things: putting an end to injustice and oppression, sharing food with the hungry, offering hospitality to the homeless, clothing the naked. Doing justice is a spiritual discipline; social witness is as fundamental as prayer in a believer's life.

This is not a "typical" book on spirituality. You will find no prayer techniques or breathing exercises or guided imagery here. The book contains no easy steps to inner peace or outer success. Rather, it is a reflection on the hard work of following Jesus Christ—and the abundant spiritual rewards that such commitment brings. I believe that we deepen our knowledge of Christ and our need for prayer as we engage with the world's suffering. Confession, thanksgiving, and intercession take on a new urgency as we place our lives among those who are vulnerable.

Over the past two decades, I have been an activist for peace concerns and a journalist covering struggles for justice in the United States and around the globe. I have worked as a court advocate for battered women, a teacher and mentor for inner-city youth, a pastor to prisoners and prostitutes and terminally ill children. It has been my honor to be invited to share the despair and the hope of people who suffer. My life has been enriched beyond measure. I have witnessed Christ crucified—and resurrected—in brothers and sisters who have opened their hearts and their lives to me. These pages contain many of their stories; I offer them as a witness to what is possible and as an invitation to continuing conversion.

The book is grounded in scripture. I believe that we cannot read the Bible without drawing the conclusion that God calls us to be involved in the work of justice. Passages about oppression, sacrificial living, and compassion for the poor appear far more often than exhortations about piety and personal practices, which have become the preoccupation of so much of Christianity today. The preaching of the prophets against economic injustice, the witness of Christ's life among the outcasts and his love for the poor, and the radical sharing of the early church all stand as testimony for believers today.

Centuries ago, Micah was called to proclaim the truth of God. As with all the prophets, Micah's anger and anguish reflected the passion of a God who rages and weeps as a parent over the suffering of his or her children. Like Isaiah, Micah preached that religious worship without social justice was meaningless. His most oft-quoted words from Micah 6:8 endure as a concise and compelling description of the life to which God calls believers:

> What does the Lord require of you
> but to do justice, and to love kindness,
> and to walk humbly with your God?

Our compassionate efforts toward justice guarantee a deepened faith and prayer life. They will lead us to disciplines of the spirit and of the heart. By engaging with suffering, we learn true joy. By touching despair, we discover what it means to embrace hope. By coming to know Christ crucified, we participate in his resurrection. By pouring ourselves out, we gain our lives.

The abundant and exquisite imagery from Isaiah 58 frames the chapters of this book, which is a reflection on the marks of engaged spirituality. The promise that awaits God's compassionate servants is a rich and exciting one: "If you...satisfy the needs of the afflicted, then shall your light rise in the darkness." May we all be beacons of hope in a world that desperately needs our witness of light and life.

Justice

To Undo the Thongs of the Yoke

IT WAS A FRIGID CHRISTMAS EVE IN WASHINGTON, D.C. In the foyer of the church that served as an overnight shelter was a gathering of shopping carts and bags loaded with years' worth of collected string, cans, broken umbrellas, and other street items. The women who owned them were finishing a sparse dinner of soup and bread.

From a corner of the fellowship hall, a lone voice began singing "Joy to the World" slightly off-key. Before long, other voices joined in; the circle of ragged women made their way through "O Come, All Ye Faithful" and "Silent Night." Most of them hadn't sung carols in years; some cried, their memories awakened to better days when they spent holidays with family and friends.

As the singing died away, the women slowly began pulling mats into place on the floor as they prepared to settle in for the night. When the lights were turned out, I took a chair in a corner next to Doris, whose asthma forced her to sleep sitting up. Her head slumped forward as she nodded off. The sound of her regular, labored breathing was the only break in the quiet of the evening for quite a while.

But sometime after midnight a disturbance erupted in the far corner. It began quietly, but before long the voices escalated into a shouting match. The argument was over a coat. Sheila accused Mary of stealing her coat while she slept. Mary jumped to her own defense, accusing Sheila of being a liar and calling her names that amounted to a long string of synonyms for "prostitute."

Sheila told Mary she was a "no-good good-for-nothing." Mary responded without hesitation, "Oh yeah? I'm better than you'll ever be. I'm an aristocrat of the highest order—with the Rothschilds on my mother's side and the Three Wise Men on my father's!"

End of discussion. Sheila couldn't top that.

SCRIPTURE

In those days Mary set out and went with haste to a Judean town in the hill country, where she entered the house of Zechariah and greeted Elizabeth. When Elizabeth heard Mary's greeting, the child leaped in her womb. And Elizabeth was filled with the Holy Spirit and exclaimed with a loud cry, "Blessed are you among women, and blessed is the fruit of your womb."

And Mary said,
"My soul magnifies the Lord,
    and my spirit rejoices in God my Savior,
    for he has looked with favor on
        the lowliness of his servant.

. . . .

He has shown strength with his arm;
    he has scattered the proud in the thoughts
        of their hearts.
He has brought down the powerful from their thrones,
    and lifted up the lowly;
he has filled the hungry with good things,
    and sent the rich away empty."

                                    ⇾ Luke 1:39-42, 46-48a, 51-53

Then Jesus, filled with the power of the Spirit, returned to Galilee, and a report about him spread through all the surrounding country. He began to teach in their synagogues and was praised by everyone.

When he came to Nazareth, where he had been brought up, he went to the synagogue on the sabbath day, as was his custom. He stood up to read, and the scroll of the prophet Isaiah was given to him. He unrolled the scroll and found the place where it was written:

"The Spirit of the Lord is upon me,
    because he has anointed me to bring good news
        to the poor.
He has sent me to proclaim release to the captives
    and recovery of sight to the blind,
        to let the oppressed go free,
to proclaim the year of the Lord's favor."

And he rolled up the scroll, gave it back to the attendant, and sat down. The eyes of all in the synagogue were fixed on him. Then he began to say to them, "Today this scripture has been fulfilled in your hearing."

↠ Luke 4:14-21

Then he looked up at his disciples and said:

"Blessed are you who are poor,
    for yours is the kingdom of God.
Blessed are you who are hungry now,
    for you will be filled.
Blessed are you who weep now,
    for you will laugh

      . . . .
But woe to you who are rich,
    for you have received your consolation.
Woe to you who are full now,
    for you will be hungry.
Woe to you who are laughing now,
    for you will mourn and weep."

↠ Luke 6:20-21, 24-25

REFLECTION

Jesus' mother knew the secret even before his birth. This child Mary carried in her womb would bring salvation to sinners and light to those in darkness. But his arrival would carry consequences far beyond the personal. Mary's song of praise reflected radical social upheaval; it was about the poor being uplifted and the powerful losing their thrones.

Mary herself was evidence of the truth of this message. To be a woman in a patriarchal society, a Jew under Roman occupation, and a peasant in a land of plenty gave Mary a social place of paramount insignificance. Yet this most unlikely vessel—a poor, Jewish woman in occupied Palestine—was chosen to bear the gift for which the world longed.

Three decades later in his hometown sermon, Jesus announced that he was the embodiment of justice. The Spirit gave him a mission: to proclaim good news to the poor and freedom to the prisoners, to break the yokes of oppression. It was a theme as old as the prophets and as intimate as the whispered lullabies of his mother. This Messiah came to open eyes: to make the physically blind see and the spiritually blind know the sin of their wealth and exploitation.

He spoke of "the year of the Lord's favor," a reference to the year of jubilee, described in Leviticus 25:8-12. To be observed every fifty years, it was a time when slaves were freed, debts were forgiven, and the land's abundance was shared. It was, in essence, a year when justice reigned and compassion ruled. Jesus, by his choice of scripture, announced at the outset of his ministry that his work was about healing, liberation, and equality. He proclaimed the inauguration of a kingdom that would fulfill all the prophetic longings for justice for those who suffered and were oppressed.

This native son awed the crowd in the synagogue: "All spoke well of him and were amazed at the gracious words that came from his mouth" (Luke 4:22). But the tone changed abruptly. When Jesus started preaching the inclusiveness of his kingdom and referred to times of God's judgment in Israel's history, the crowd turned on him. The proud and smiling hometown folks suddenly were "filled with rage." They "drove him out of the town, and led him to the brow of the hill...so that they might hurl him off the cliff" (4:28-29). Jesus' message was unsettling, to say the least; it rattled the status quo.

Telling the truth of America today is as unsettling as it was to tell the truth of Israel then. Over thirty-six million Americans live in poverty. One in four children in the United States is poor, and infant mortality rates in our inner cities rival those of developing countries. Domestic violence is the leading cause of injury to women: Three million women are beaten each year, and every day four women are murdered by their partners or husbands. Homicide is the leading cause of death among young African-American men, and more are in prison or on parole than in college. AIDS, drug addiction, and suicide lay claim to more and more citizens, including an alarming number of youth. Hundreds of thousands of Americans are homeless and unemployed as affordable housing evaporates and corporations ship jobs to foreign countries that pay workers pennies a day.

Rampant patriotic fervor and shouts of "God bless America" can't drown out the cries behind the reality of our nation. For those of us who claim to follow Jesus Christ—the one who came to open eyes—looking away is not an option. Jesus invites us to participate in the coming of God's kingdom.

From one coast to the other, I've observed struggles for justice up close. On the sea islands off the coast of South Carolina, descendants of slaves are trying to stave off the development of luxury resorts that are robbing them of their land and homes. Medical workers in Washington, D.C., live in community with homeless men infected with HIV or suffering from AIDS, offering compassionate care and advocating the rights of those treated as our nation's outcasts. In the scattered communities of Virginia's Appalachian hills, miners and their families have gone on strike against millionaire corporate executives who took away health benefits from men suffering and dying from black lung and other mine-related disabilities.

Detroit mothers who lost children in street violence have formed SOSAD (Save Our Sons and Daughters), working for gun control and an end to the illegal drug trade that propels the mayhem. Residents downwind of the Nevada Nuclear Test Site battle for compensation for the cancers and other radiation-related illnesses that plague their communities. Across the land, Christians are welcoming refugees and caring for abused children, visiting prisoners and offering shelter to battered women.

My friend Mary at the overnight shelter suffers from mental illness. She, like thousands of others, was put out on the street years ago when the government emptied many state mental hospitals and other institutions. For most of her life, Mary has been told that she is worthless. But that Christmas Eve in the shelter, in her own bizarre way, she commandeered some dignity for herself. She claimed royalty in her bloodline. And in some sense that night, the rich were dethroned and the poor were exalted.

Mary's claim echoed the centuries-old song of the other Mary, the mother of Jesus. The message was clear: Change is coming. Everything's about to turn upside down. The question for us is, Which side are we on?

FOR PRAYER AND DISCUSSION

1. What is my response to Jesus' words: "Today this scripture has been fulfilled"?

2. In what ways does my living further the kingdom or uphold the status quo?

3. In what ways do my home life, work, and prayer reflect Jesus' invitation to embrace justice?

Compassion

To Share Your Bread with the Hungry

DURING MY FIFTEEN YEARS IN WASHINGTON, I helped give out food on Saturday mornings at the Sojourners Neighborhood Center. People still refer to the area of the center's location as the Fourteenth Street "riot corridor," three decades after violence swept the city following the assassination of Dr. Martin Luther King, Jr. It still bears the scars: vacant lots and abandoned buildings, broken glass and shattered hopes.

Every Saturday up to three hundred families came through the food line for a bag of groceries. Before opening the line, those of us serving the food clasped hands and bowed our heads. Mary Glover, an older neighborhood resident who had lived there for decades, offered a prayer. It was the same prayer every week, but it never seemed redundant. I will carry it with me always :

> We thank you, Lord, for our lying down last night and our rising up this morning. We thank you that the walls of our room were not the walls of our grave, that our bed was not our cooling board nor our bedclothes our winding-sheet. We thank you for the feet that are coming through this line for food today and the hands that are giving it out. We know, Lord, that you're coming through this line today, so help us to treat you right. Yes, Lord, help us to treat you right.

SCRIPTURE

When the Son of Man comes in his glory, and all the angels with him, then he will sit on the throne of his glory. All the nations will be gathered before him, and he will separate people one from another as a shepherd separates the sheep from the goats, and he will put the sheep at his right hand and the goats at the left.

Then the king will say to those at his right hand, "Come, you that are blessed by my Father, inherit the kingdom prepared for you from the foundation of the world; for I was hungry and you gave me food, I was thirsty and you gave me something to drink, I was a stranger and you welcomed me, I was naked and you gave me clothing, I was sick and you took care of me, I was in prison and you visited me."

Then the righteous will answer him, "Lord, when was it that we saw you hungry and gave you food, or thirsty and gave you something to drink? And when was it that we saw you a stranger and welcomed you, or naked and gave you clothing? And when was it that we saw you sick or in prison and visited you?"

And the king will answer them, "Truly I tell you, just as you did it to one of the least of these who are members of my family, you did it to me."

Then he will say to those at his left hand, "You that are accursed, depart from me into the eternal fire prepared for the devil and his angels; for I was hungry and you gave me no food, I was thirsty and you gave me nothing to drink, I was a stranger and you did not welcome me, naked and you did not give me clothing, sick and in prison and you did not visit me."

Then they also will answer, "Lord, when was it that we saw you hungry or thirsty or a stranger or naked or sick or in prison, and did not take care of you?"

Then he will answer them, "Truly I tell you, just as you did not do it to one of the least of these, you did not do it to me." And these will go away into eternal punishment, but the righteous into eternal life.

➔ Matthew 25:31-46

There was a rich man who was dressed in purple and fine linen and who feasted sumptuously every day. And at his gate lay a poor man named Lazarus, covered with sores, who longed to satisfy his hunger with what fell from the rich man's table; even the dogs would come and lick his sores.

The poor man died and was carried away by the angels to be with Abraham. The rich man also died and was buried. In Hades, where he was being tormented, he looked up and saw Abraham far away with Lazarus by his side. He called out, "Father Abraham, have mercy on me, and send Lazarus to dip the tip of his finger in water and cool my tongue; for I am in agony in these flames."

But Abraham said, "Child, remember that during your lifetime you received your good things, and Lazarus in like manner evil things; but now he is comforted here, and you are in agony. Besides all this, between you and us a great chasm has been fixed, so that those who might want to pass from here to you cannot do so, and no one can cross from there to us."

He said, "Then, father, I beg you to send him to my father's house—for I have five brothers—that he may warn them, so that they will not also come into this place of torment." Abraham replied, "They have Moses and the prophets; they should listen to them." He said, "No, father Abraham; but if someone goes to them from the dead, they will repent." He said to him, "If they do not listen to Moses and the prophets, neither will they be convinced even if someone rises from the dead."

➔ Luke 16:19-31

What good is it, my brothers and sisters, if you say you have faith but do not have works? Can faith save you? If a brother or sister is naked and lacks daily food, and one of you says to them, "Go in peace; keep warm and eat your fill," and yet you do not supply their bodily needs, what is the good of that? So faith by itself, if it has no works, is dead.

→ James 2:14-17

REFLECTION

The Luke 4 passage from our previous chapter, which recounts Jesus' reading in the synagogue, and his words above from Matthew 25 provide a striking frame for his ministry. The first serves as Jesus' inauguration speech; the second describes the end of his mission—his expected second coming. Here Jesus sits on his throne in glory, judging the nations. He applies one criterion for their salvation or damnation: how they treated people in need. Did they feed the hungry, welcome the strangers, visit the sick and imprisoned? If so, salvation is theirs; if not, eternal doom.

But Jesus says even more in Matthew 25. He tells us where we can find him. To serve a suffering sister or brother is to serve Jesus. He is there in the prisons and the soup lines, in the shelters and the refugee camps, on the streets and the hospital wards. We cannot follow Jesus if we refuse to go where he is. Our salvation is at stake, dependent on how we treat the "least of these."

Mary Glover knew the truth of Matthew 25. She knew that she was serving her Lord every time she handed out a loaf of bread. She treated each person in that food line with dignity and respect—as a son or daughter of God.

Jesus' command in these verses is a starting place. It's an invitation to move away from the paralysis that often comes when facing the overwhelming nature of the world's suffering. Start with one hungry person, one homeless family, one teenager with a problem pregnancy, one neighbor with cancer. Go—and meet Jesus.

To share a loaf of bread is a radical act. In the verses imme-

diately following the Matthew 25 passage, Jesus announces that
he will be crucified, and the chief priests and elders gather in
the palace of the high priest, where they "conspired to arrest
Jesus by stealth and kill him" (Matt. 26:4). Words of truth pro-
voked violence against Jesus both at the beginning and at the
end of his ministry.

Jesus had the audacity to preach that the hungry should
receive food and the sick receive care. And he had the courage
to make his home among the outcasts of his day: the lame, the
blind, the lepers, the prostitutes, and the beggars.

In the late 1970s and into the 1980s, when war was raging
in Central America, streams of refugees made their way to this
country. Many were Christian "delegates of the Word," peasant
leaders who took the Bible's promise of justice seriously. In
Guatemala and El Salvador, a tiny minority of wealthy elites—
many supported by U.S. corporations and military interests—
controlled the land and the resources, while the vast majority of
the people went hungry. Efforts to bring justice were met with
brutal repression: torture, murder, and "disappearances." In El
Salvador alone, 75,000 people were killed in a decade, including an archbishop, several priests, and four U.S. missionary women.

Fleeing the terror at home, refugees risked their lives to cross
the borders into the southwestern U.S. A "sanctuary movement"
grew up among churches here to meet their needs for shelter,
food, clothing, and transportation to Canada, where many were
granted asylum. The U.S. government declared the churches' compassion illegal. Many sanctuary workers were arrested; some
served time in jail.

Jack Elder faced the charge of "transporting illegal aliens."
Rev. Donovan Cook served as a witness on Elder's behalf, and he
referred to Matthew 25's mandate to care for the poor. The judge,
himself a Christian, said that of course the Bible talks about feeding and clothing and visiting the needy, but it "says nothing
about transporting them."

Referring to Luke 10:25-37, Cook reminded the judge of the parable of the Good Samaritan:

> Just then a lawyer stood up to test Jesus. "Teacher," he said, "what must I do to inherit eternal life?" He said to him, "What is written in the law? What do you read there?" He answered, "You shall love the Lord your God with all your heart, and with all your soul, and with all your strength, and with all your mind; and your neighbor as yourself." And he said to him, "You have given the right answer; do this, and you will live."
>
> But wanting to justify himself, he asked Jesus, "And who is my neighbor?" Jesus replied, "A man was going down from Jerusalem to Jericho, and fell into the hands of robbers, who stripped him, beat him, and went away, leaving him half dead. Now by chance a priest was going down that road; and when he saw him, he passed on the other side. So likewise a Levite, when he came to the place and saw him, passed by on the other side.
>
> But a Samaritan while traveling came near him; and when he saw him, he was moved with pity. He went to him and bandaged his wounds, having poured oil and wine on them. Then he put him on his own animal, brought him to an inn, and took care of him. The next day he took out two denarii, gave them to the innkeeper, and said, 'Take care of him; and when I come back, I will repay you whatever more you spend.' Which of these three, do you think, was a neighbor to the man who fell into the hands of robbers?" He said, "The one who showed him mercy." Jesus said to him, "Go and do likewise."

"So you see," said Cook to the judge, "the good Samaritan found a suffering man in the road, bound up his wounds, put him on his beast, and *transported* him to the nearest shelter."

WHO IS OUR NEIGHBOR TODAY? Who needs our compassion?

Matthew 25 is about nations, Luke 16 about individuals. The story of the rich man and Lazarus graphically portrays the cost of isolation from those who suffer. The one who chooses to be isolated in this life will also be isolated in the next—on the other side of a "great chasm" that cannot be breached. The testimony of Jesus and the prophets is an exhortation to compassion. Those who do not listen pay an eternal price.

Children are hungry; women are wounded; racism stalks the land. And Jesus sits on his throne in glory and asks us, "Did you feed me? Did you clothe me? Did you visit me?" He cries from the streets and the borders, "Will you welcome me?"

Dorothy Day, a founder of Catholic Worker Houses of Hospitality during the Great Depression, called acts of compassion toward the poor the "works of mercy." She wrote at the end of her autobiography, *The Long Loneliness*:

> We were just sitting there talking when lines of people began to form, saying, "We need bread." We could not say, "Go, be thou filled." If there were six small loaves and a few fishes, we had to divide them. There was always bread.

From her simple acts of sharing bread and shelter grew a movement founded on compassion and service. Catholic Worker Houses have been opening doors for more than half a century.

The lines are swelling again. We all can hand out bread. We all can visit the sick. These acts should be as natural to us as prayer, part of our routine of faithfulness. Compassion is intercession incarnate.

When we serve those in need, we follow Jesus who proclaimed good news to the poor, who lived among the most desperate and despised. The hungry child, the homeless man, the frightened refugee all wait. Go—and meet Jesus.

FOR PRAYER AND DISCUSSION

1. In whom do I see the face of Jesus?

2. How can I embrace a spiritual discipline that serves "the least of these"?

3. How can I "put flesh" on my intercessory prayers?

Confession

Remove the Pointing of the Finger

I N 1981, A NUCLEAR WEAPONS exposition came to a Washington hotel. Many Christians felt that it was an affront for this "arms bazaar" to come to our city, particularly when funds for food stamps and school lunches were drying up. Hunger was at a record high in D.C. at a time when the Pentagon was bloated.

About 250 people gathered outside the hotel one evening while an elegant military dinner took place inside. We sang and prayed. Then fifty of us, each with a loaf of bread, sat in the hotel's driveway under a banner that proclaimed "Bread, Not Bombs." During our arrest, our offense of blocking the driveway was recorded officially as "incommoding."

We spent the night in two large holding cells under the D.C courthouse, one for the women and one for the men. The cell across the corridor from ours was filled with women swept up in a raid on a local house of prostitution. Shouting through the bars, I conversed for a long time with a young woman named Gloria.

Gloria told me she had made a lot of mistakes in her life. She saw her arrest as a sign that she needed to make some changes, especially since she had a young son to care for. With a gleam of hope in her eyes, she said, "God always gives us second chances."

About 3 o'clock in the morning, we decided to try to get some sleep. I stretched out on the cold, concrete floor, gripping a contact lens in each fist. A short time later a loud racket awakened me. In the dim light with my blurry vision, I just barely made out the form of a large woman with a huge heart tattooed on her arm. As she was let into the cell across from ours, she nodded our way and shouted, "What did *they* do to get in here?" I heard Gloria respond with a giggle, "They incommoded!" Then she added, "At a hotel!"

Around dawn a few of the women in our cell began to sing, and others soon joined in, shaking off a stiff drowsiness. Gloria shouted over to us, "Hey, do you all know 'Amazing Grace'?" Soon strains of the hymn thundered through the corridor as the two sides of the cell block tried to outsing each other:

> Amazing grace! How sweet the sound
> that saved a wretch like me!

I decided it was time to put my contact lenses back in my eyes. I groped blindly toward the chrome contraption that served as drinking fountain, sink, and toilet for our cell. Searching for water for my lenses, I pushed what I thought was the tap for the sink. The deafening roar of the jail toilet immediately silenced the singing. Laughing and pointing at me from across the corridor, Gloria hollered, "Now, *that's* incommoding!"

Soon everyone was laughing. Then Gloria started "Amazing Grace" again:

> I once was lost, but now am found;
> was blind, but now I see.

Before long a guard came to investigate all the commotion and try to silence us.

"What's going on?" he asked brusquely.

Gloria jumped up and pressed her face against the bars. Looking the guard squarely in the eyes, she declared, "It's only the *gospel*."

SCRIPTURE

Early in the morning [Jesus] came again to the temple. All the people came to him and he sat down and began to teach them.

The scribes and the Pharisees brought a woman who had been caught in adultery; and making her stand before all of them, they said to him, "Teacher, this woman was caught in the very act of committing adultery. Now in the law Moses commanded us to stone such women. Now what do you say?" They said this to test him, that they might have some charge to bring against him.

Jesus bent down and wrote with his finger on the ground. When they kept on questioning him, he straightened up and said to them, "Let anyone among you who is without sin be the first to throw a stone at her." And once again he bent down and wrote on the ground.

When they heard it, they went away, one by one, beginning with the elders; and Jesus was left alone with the woman standing before him. Jesus straightened up and said to her, "Woman, where are they? Has no one condemned you?"

She said, "No one, sir."

And Jesus said, "Neither do I condemn you. Go your way, and from now on do not sin again."

➔ John 8:2-11

[Jesus] also told this parable to some who trusted in themselves that they were righteous and regarded others with contempt: "Two men went up to the temple to pray, one a Pharisee and the other a tax collector. The Pharisee, standing by himself, was praying thus, 'God, I thank you that I am not like other people: thieves, rogues, adulterers, or even like this tax collector. I fast twice a week; I give a tenth of all my income.' But the tax collector, standing far off, would not even look up to heaven, but was beating his breast and saying, 'God, be merciful to me a sinner!' I tell you, this man went down to his home justified rather than the other; for all who exalt themselves will be humbled, but all who humble themselves will be exalted."

↪ Luke 18:9-14

This is the message we have heard from him and proclaim to you, that God is light and in him there is no darkness at all. If we say that we have fellowship with him while we are walking in darkness, we lie and do not do what is true; but if we walk in the light as he himself is in the light, we have fellowship with one another, and the blood of Jesus his Son cleanses us from all sin. If we say that we have no sin, we deceive ourselves, and the truth is not in us. If we confess our sins, he who is faithful and just will forgive us our sins and cleanse us from all unrighteousness. If we say that we have not sinned, we make him a liar, and his word is not in us.

↪ 1 John 1:5-9

REFLECTION

I learned some of my most profound spiritual lessons in jail. I carry with me a collection of memories of women who taught me over the years, memories gleaned from several return visits to the D.C. jail.

Sylvia, three months pregnant when I met her, was a heroin addict. Her cell was a few doors down and across the corridor from mine. Her hands were all that I could see of her. They alternately dangled limply and trembled as she spoke about her abusive father, her escape from home and into drugs, and how much she wanted her baby. She spent a night moaning and pounding the walls—overcome with the agony of heroin withdrawal—while the rest of us on the cell block tried futilely to get the attention of the prison guards by shouting and rattling our cell bars.

Wanda always looked down and kept her arms folded, trying to hide cigarette burns on her face and hands. Her father had burned and sexually abused her as a child. She had been trying to hustle a living on the streets, with little success. Wanda sucked her thumb when she slept at night on her bunk.

Tamika had been thrown out of her home by her father when she was fourteen. She entertained the cell block with her description of trying to cash a check at a bank. Tamika had found the check, written to a Sally Harvey, on the street: "The bank teller told me that Sally Harvey was a tall Caucasian with blonde hair. I told myself, 'Uh-oh.'"

Shirley, who had been arrested for prostitution, said that as a child she had squeezed a tube of toothpaste into her baby brother's ear. "I guess I've just always been bad," she concluded.

THE WOMEN I MET IN JAIL were victims of sexism and racism, of sorely lacking financial and emotional resources. Government priorities excluded them, and politicians and bureaucrats wished they would go away (as some of their families had wished since the day of their birth). And they were victims of their own bad choices.

They wept for their children and vowed to make their lives better. They tried to shed addictions and find work—often failing—but picking themselves up and trying again. They taught me about God's grace and about being given second chances—and third and fourth chances. That was the most profound lesson of all.

The phrase *widows and orphans*—meaning women and children without the support of men—appears throughout the Bible as the paradigm of powerlessness and vulnerability. The ancient Israelites were commanded to care for them, and collections were taken on their behalf in the early Christian church.

The situation hasn't changed much in several thousand years, as women on their own or solely responsible for children are slipping into poverty at an alarming rate. Desperation sometimes pushes them to sell illegal drugs, pass bad checks, or peddle their bodies.

The Book of Ruth in the Hebrew Scriptures records the story of Ruth and Naomi, two women who had to fend for themselves after their husbands' deaths. Consigned to the life of the poor, Ruth gleaned among the grain left by the harvesters in the fields and, with Naomi, subsisted on the leftovers of the socially secure. Hebrew law demanded that harvesters leave gleanings for "the poor and the alien" (Leviticus 19:9; 23:22) or "the alien, the orphan, and the widow" (Deuteronomy 24:19). In other words, the charity of gleanings was a "safety net" offered to those whom the system had failed, the ones who had fallen through the cracks and were left bereft of other options for survival.

What a contrast we find today. Contempt is rife for "the alien, the orphan, and the widow." Even the crumbs and gleanings are being denied to the needy. The city of Phoenix, Arizona, has declared that all garbage is city property. People found scavenging for food can be arrested; the poor can go to jail for breaking and entering a city Dumpster for a loaf of outdated bread or a piece of bruised fruit. Atlanta, Georgia—in the face of burgeoning downtown development and the arrival of the 1996 Olympic Games—announced a campaign for a "vagrant-free zone," enforced by harassment and arrest of the homeless poor for such offenses as walking across a parking lot in which they have no car parked. Other cities have built sharp wire cages over steam grates to keep the homeless from sleeping there for warmth in the winter, essentially declaring heat a commodity only for those able to pay for it.

The prophet Isaiah called for an end to "the pointing of the finger," a gesture of blame and contempt toward the poor. He may as well have been speaking directly to us. "Criminals," "illegal aliens," and "welfare mothers" are being scapegoated for a variety of national ills. While schools decay and job training programs disappear for lack of funds, prisons are a growth industry. The U.S. prison population doubled in the decade from 1985 to 1995 under harsher sentencing laws; the "crackdown on crime" has affected youth especially.

Razor wire runs rampant along our southern border in an effort to deter immigrants, while those who have already made it to this country are being denied medical and educational services. What little safety net there was in place for women and children (flawed as it is) is being dismantled, with no secure means of survival replacing it.

We would do well to remember that we follow a Savior who was born of a poor mother, lived for a time as a refugee in Egypt, and was condemned to death as a criminal.

We need to take Isaiah's words to heart, reminding ourselves once again that we are all children of God. As Matthew 25 makes clear, not only our well-being as a nation but our very souls are at stake. Jesus never stopped and asked who deserved compassion. He demanded no proof of effort or righteousness or worth. He simply served and healed—the lame, the blind, the outcasts, the sinners.

This is good news not just for the poor but for us all. Our culture encourages us to believe that being a success and "making it on our own" is a virtue. Our nation cheerleads for winners.

But most of us don't feel like winners much of the time. For many of us, life hasn't turned out exactly as we had hoped. Perhaps a divorce, an unresolved conflict with a family member, loss of a job, a child in trouble, a debilitating illness, a bout with loneliness, or some other unexpected turn of events has left us feeling less than successful, perhaps even overwhelmed by grief or despair. Ours is a nation full of unfulfilling jobs, loveless marriages, and estranged families. Yet we don't have many clues as to how to face our weakness or failure; we receive coaching in how to hide the aspects of our lives that are less than positive.

But the testimony of scripture offers a different picture. Jesus told several parables about sin and loss. The parable of the lost sheep ends with the proclamation that "there will be more joy in heaven over one sinner who repents than over ninety-nine righteous persons who need no repentance" (Luke 15:7).

Similarly, the parable of the lost coin concludes, "There is joy in the presence of the angels of God over one sinner who repents" (Luke 15:10).

The parable of the prodigal son immediately follows these. When I read this story, I identify most with the jealous older brother. I'm sure I would be whining outside the party. I would have resented staying home, working hard, and being a good son while my brother sinned and squandered—and he gets the fine robe and the fatted calf. But we have to celebrate and rejoice, explains the father, "because this brother of yours was dead and has come to life; he was lost and has been found" (Luke 15:32).

Luke 7:36-50 recounts a meal that Jesus shared in the house of a Pharisee: "A woman in the city, who was a sinner"—a prostitute—came and knelt at Jesus' feet, bathing them with her tears and anointing them with ointment. The Pharisee was scandalized that Jesus would allow such a woman to touch him. Jesus responded by telling the parable of the two debtors and ended by saying of the woman: "Her sins, which were many, have been forgiven; hence she has shown great love. But the one to whom little is forgiven, loves little."

The women I met in jail are kin to this woman. They, like the woman caught in adultery, know what forgiveness and salvation are all about. Their most obvious sins, born of desperation, reflect the sins of those of us who are complacent or uncaring toward their plight.

We must confess a lack of will in this self-proclaimed Christian nation to guarantee the dignity and well-being of all our citizens. As others have already proclaimed, the moral fabric of our nation is unraveling—not simply because divorce rates are spiraling and popular music and television programs showcase random violence and sex. We also seem to have lost our moorings, our sense of responsibility for one another. We seem to have forgotten that our destinies are intertwined, that the well-being of one depends on the well-being of all.

Conjecture has gone on for centuries about what Jesus wrote in the sand during the episode with the woman caught in adultery. Perhaps he was just scribbling aimlessly, thinking through his answer and buying time while the scribes and Pharisees watched, letting them know he wasn't rattled by their attempt to verbally trap him. Or maybe he was writing words like *pride*, *hypocrisy*, and *self-righteousness*. Maybe the obsessive keepers of the law were being forced to read a list of their own sins traced in the dust.

With one statement, Jesus took the vengeful wind out of the accusers' sails: "Let anyone among you who is without sin be the first to throw a stone at her" (John 8:7). No one moved. Then slowly, one by one, the stones dropped and the crowd walked off, the elders leading the way. They were all guilty—of using this woman as a scapegoat, if nothing else.

In Matthew 23:23-24 Jesus declares, "Woe to you, scribes and Pharisees, hypocrites! For you tithe mint, dill, and cummin, and have neglected the weightier matters of the law: justice and mercy and faith.... You strain out a gnat but swallow a camel!"

Jesus addressed these words to those preoccupied with righteousness according to the law. They calculated every tithe, down to the smallest spice and herb. But they ignored the demands of the big picture: justice and mercy and faith. They knew little about God's grace.

Faith without works may be dead, as James exhorts us, but our works will not save us: "All have sinned and fallen short of the glory of God; they are now justified by his grace as a gift, through the redemption that is in Christ Jesus" (Romans 3:23-24).

> For by grace you have been saved through faith, and this is not your own doing; it is the gift of God—not the result of works, so that no one may boast. For we are what he has made us, created in Christ Jesus for good works, which God prepared beforehand to be our way of life.
>
> ↳ Ephesians 2:8-10

Gloria knew exactly what she was talking about when she answered that guard. She is a woman who knows that a generous and forgiving God sustains her. She understands the power of amazing grace. And she opened my eyes to another dimension of what it means to see the gospel as good news.

Gloria finds hope in the story of the prodigal son. As the parable makes clear, we don't always get what we deserve. Thank God.

FOR PRAYER AND DISCUSSION

1. What do I need to confess?
2. How do I experience the truth of God's grace?
3. How do my relationships and attitudes toward others mirror God's generosity and forgiveness toward me?

Surrender

To Pour Yourself Out

AN EERIE WAIL PUNCTURED OUR SILENT prayer as the Sojourners Community gathered for worship on Ash Wednesday, 1991. The siren wailed on and on, seemingly without end, and sent a disturbing jolt through the room. Our prayer focus was a war thousands of miles away, and the siren added poignant urgency to our petitions. *It must be like this in Baghdad,* I thought: *the night full of frightening sounds—and over there, deadly fire.* I thought of the children.

The disturbance in Washington, D.C., that night was a malfunctioning civil defense siren. Panicked residents flooded local police precincts with calls trying to find out if Iraq had launched a terrorist attack on the capital city. I went home to watch the local news on TV: I learned that U.S. forces had just bombed the Amariya shelter in Baghdad, killing hundreds of Iraqi women and children.

I stayed awake late into the night, kept awake by other sirens—sirens of police cars or ambulances, the sounds of a drug raid or another shooting in the neighborhood. I felt despair overtaking me as I thought about the war across the globe and the one right outside the window. Personally, it was a time of loneliness for me, of seemingly irresolvable conflict with people I loved. I tried to pray but found that I couldn't.

I got up and built an altar that night beneath my collection of images of "Madonna and Child" from places around the globe—from South Africa and Russia, from Appalachia, the Navajo Nation, and the streets of my own city. I covered the altar with a Palestinian scarf brought back by a friend from a trip to the Middle East. I added stones and sand and candles, images of desert and light.

I built my altar as an act of faith in a time of gnawing emptiness. And I decided that night as I knelt before it—when the words to pray wouldn't come—to keep a fast through Lent. It was a discipline I had never embraced before—an act to stave off a spiral of despair, a choice when there seemed to be no other.

Several days into my water-and-juice fast I began to notice that I was looking at the world differently. I sensed a sharpness of vision and a deepened awareness of the presence of God. When my physical strength gave out, the assurance of God's sustenance took powerful hold. In my despair, I needed such a sign. But still I remained closed to part of God's power.

I couldn't escape it in the desert. Three weeks into my fast, I went to a protest vigil at the Nevada Test Site, where our nation explodes its nuclear weapons. After a liturgy for peace with a crowd at the edge of the test site, I wandered off to be alone. I went to a place where there were just myself, the gravelly sand, and an occasional Joshua tree with spiny leaves and branches outstretched like arms toward God.

There, as other pilgrims to the desert have done for centuries, I fell to my knees and discovered an emptiness beyond any I had ever known. For the first time in weeks, I was able to weep, to allow my tears to spill and water the barren earth.

And in pouring out the despair, I found room for something I had been closed to since Ash Wednesday. There, on the twenty-fourth day of my fast, the words of a gentle God fed me, and I found hope:

I am about to do a new thing;
>   now it springs forth, do you not perceive it?
I will make a way in the wilderness
>   and rivers in the desert

. . . .

to give drink to my chosen people.

>   ✦ Isaiah 43:19-20

SCRIPTURE

Jesus, full of the Holy Spirit, returned from the Jordan and was led by the Spirit in the wilderness, where for forty days he was tempted by the devil. He ate nothing at all during those days, and when they were over, he was famished. The devil said to him, "If you are the Son of God, command this stone to become a loaf of bread." Jesus answered him, "It is written, 'One does not live by bread alone.'"

Then the devil led him up and showed him in an instant all the kingdoms of the world. And the devil said to him, "To you I will give their glory and all this authority; for it has been given over to me, and I give it to anyone I please. If you, then, will worship me, it will all be yours." Jesus answered him, "It is written,

'Worship the Lord your God,
>   and serve only him.'"

Then the devil took him to Jerusalem, and placed him on the pinnacle of the temple, saying to him, "If you are the Son of God, throw yourself down from here, for it is written,

'He will command his angels concerning you,
>   to protect you,'

and

'On their hands they will bear you up,
>   so that you will not dash your
>   foot against a stone.'"

Jesus answered him, "It is said, 'Do not put the Lord your

God to the test.'" When the devil had finished every test, he departed from him until an opportune time.

→ Luke 4:1-13

Then someone came to [Jesus] and said, "Teacher, what good deed must I do to have eternal life?" And he said to him, "Why do you ask me what is good?...If you wish to enter into life, keep the commandments."...The young man said to him, "I have kept all these; what do I still lack?" Jesus said to him, "If you wish to be perfect, go, sell your possessions, and give the money to the poor, and you will have treasure in heaven; then come, follow me." When the young man heard this word, he went away grieving, for he had many possessions.

→ Matthew 19:16-17, 20-22

Let each of you look not to your own interests, but to the interests of others. Let the same mind be in you that was in Christ Jesus,

who, though he was in the form of God,
did not regard equality with God
as something to be exploited,
but emptied himself,
taking the form of a slave,
being born in human likeness.
And being found in human form,
he humbled himself
and became obedient to the point of death—
even death on a cross.

→ Philippians 2:4-8

REFLECTION

The Jews awaited a Messiah. They had in mind a warrior, thundering in on a tall steed, breaking the brutal oppression of Roman occupation with a wave of his arm: an instant end to suffering, the beginning of a lasting liberation.

The Messiah who appeared was a baby born in a stable and

placed in a feeding trough; a refugee before his second birthday, in flight to Egypt to escape King Herod's wrath and his ordered massacre of baby boys. Years later, this Messiah rode into Jerusalem not on a thundering steed but on a halting donkey, the symbol of humility. He not only refused to groom the favor of the religious authorities but was the target of their scorn and hatred. He preached servant leadership and left his disciples with the example of washing one another's feet. And, ultimately, he was put to death on a cross—a method of execution for criminals in the Roman Empire. Where was the promised power? the liberation?

We see Jesus' deep integrity in the passage from Luke about his testing in the desert. Satan pulled out everything in his temptation arsenal. The devil dared Jesus, famished after a forty-day fast, to turn stones into bread. Next Satan offered him all the kingdoms of the world if Jesus simply would bow down before him. Then he took him to the pinnacle of the temple, daring Jesus to test God's power.

In various ways, these same temptations dangle before us. Our society bombards us with constant messages about the importance of meeting (and exceeding) our physical needs. It stresses financial security at the expense of spiritual growth. Cars, clothes, vacations, perfumes—even soft drinks—have become status symbols in our consumer culture.

Popular seminars teach us how to use power and influence, each promising us the world if we simply follow seven or ten or twelve easy steps in our business and personal relations. Read the right books, know the right people, get the right job—all are avenues to power and prestige in a culture obsessed by status and privilege.

But if we follow such advice, we are looking in the wrong place. Luke 3, the chapter before Jesus' temptation, begins with these words:

> In the fifteenth year of the reign of Tiberius Caesar, Pontius Pilate being governor of Judea, and Herod being tetrarch of

Galilee, and his brother Philip tetrarch of the region of Itu-
raea and Trachonitis, and Lysanias tetrarch of Abilene, in
the high priesthood of Annas and Caiaphas, the word of
God came to John the son of Zechariah in the wilderness
(vss. 1-2, RSV).

It's the sort of passage you hope you never have to read in front
of a congregation on Sunday morning—full of unpronounce-
able names and places nobody's ever heard of. And what's a
tetrarch anyway?

But this rather cumbersome overview of the political and
religious landscape makes a critical point: God could have sent
the Word to the centers of political or religious power—but
chose instead to have it come to John in the wilderness. The
punch line is meant to startle. If we want to find where the
Word is being preached, we have to go to the margins; we have
to go to the "desert."

Jesus lived that truth. He refused to abuse his power, to relin-
quish his trust in God, or to do the spectacular—for either survival or show. He emptied himself of pride and selfish concern,
so that he could be filled with the Spirit. By his choices, he
claimed that his loyalties lay with God, not with the world.

The young man in the Matthean passage made a different
choice. His possessions symbolized his loyalties. When confronted
with the truth that following Jesus was about more than following the law—and required a sacrifice of his security—the young
man abandoned the requirements of faith and went away sor-
rowful.

Motlalepula Chabaku, a pastor in exile from South Africa
for many years, offered the following reflection when I inter-
viewed her:

The church in the Western world is so steeped in materialism, in structure, that it loses people. Meanwhile, Christ
is being hurt and is crying in pain in places of hunger and
torture. Christ is alive in areas of conflict, but where peo-

ple are materially comfortable, they find it difficult to carry the cross of Christ. They have their house first, the insurance, their car, family, and after all this, they have the cross. How can they hold it with all that too?

We have nothing. We carry the cross close to us. That's why we find Christians growing in number in areas of strife and conflict: Latin America, Africa, and Asia.

It's difficult for most Christians in the United States to know emptiness or hunger. It's nearly impossible for us to take to heart Jesus' words: "If any want to become my followers, let them deny themselves and take up their cross and follow me" (Matt. 16:24; Mark 8:34; see also Luke 9:23); "Whoever does not take up the cross and follow me is not worthy of me" (Matt. 10:38) and "cannot be my disciple" (Luke 14:27).

The cross is about emptying, surrender, and sacrifice—the antithesis of the messages and symbols that drive our culture. The cross symbolizes a renunciation of the world's power and promises and an embracing of the love of God.

The cross is also about liberation—about the freedom that comes from being empty before God and completely in God's hands. This is the ultimate scandal of Jesus: that liberation is born not in grabbing power but in self-emptying. Only in pouring ourselves out can we be refilled with the spirit of God.

The disciples demanded to know who was the greatest in the kingdom of heaven. We can't know for certain whom they had in mind (perhaps each pictured himself), but we can be sure that Jesus' answer surprised them:

> He called a child, whom he put among them, and said, "Truly I tell you, unless you change and become like children, you will never enter the kingdom of heaven. Whoever becomes humble like this child is the greatest in the kingdom of heaven. Whoever welcomes one such child in my name welcomes me."
>
> → Matthew 18:2-5

Unless you change. Jesus knew well the human tendency to self-importance. His own life stood as a counterwitness. He was living proof of God's awesome, reason-defying choice to come to earth as a child, to live as an itinerant teacher and healer, and finally to go to a humiliating death on a cross. *Incarnation*: God made a self-emptying choice so that we would know not just God's cosmic power but also God's intimate love for us.

John Wesley prayed,

> I give myself completely to you, God. Assign me to my place in your creation. Let me suffer for you. Give me the work you would have me do. Give me many tasks, or have me step aside while you call others. Put me forward or humble me. Give me riches or let me live in poverty. I freely give all that I am and all that I have to you…. Amen.

FOR PRAYER AND DISCUSSION

1. Where is my "desert," the place I experience being empty before God?

2. What would it mean for me to "change and become like [a child]" in my faith life?

3. How can my prayers help me live a life of surrender to God?

Simplicity

God Will Satisfy Your Needs

N THE SUMMER OF 1983, AN ECUMENICAL delegation of 150 Christians from North Carolina visited Nicaragua's northern frontier. They discovered that U.S.-sponsored forces known as contras were raiding villages, killing and kidnapping. Terrorized Nicaraguans testified to children's being taken and entire towns massacred. But while the North Carolinians were in the area, the raids ceased.

Bringing home with them the Nicaraguans' pleas to do whatever they could to stop the "secret war," a few members of the delegation called other people of faith together. We spent a weekend talking about what could be done. We decided that if North American presence provided protection and an end to the raids, the most faithful response would be an ongoing, prayerful presence of people of faith in Nicaragua's war zones. Thus was born Witness for Peace, a nonviolent effort that spanned several years and involved thousands of U.S. witnesses to Nicaragua's pain.

In December 1983, I was a member of the first team to go to Nicaragua. We were headed by bus over an isolated road to Jalapa, a vulnerable village near the Honduran border. We got as far as the town of Ocotal and had to stop. Contra forces had been spotted in the area, and the town was put under alert. We spent the night on the floor of a Baptist church, which we shared with Nicaraguan refugees who had fled their scattered mountain homes. Most were women and young children.

It was a restless night. Children cried close at hand, and gunshots pierced the distance. We awoke before dawn and washed our faces in a rain barrel outside the church, ready to move on toward the border. The refugee women had risen even earlier. Already they had stacked firewood in their dome-shaped clay oven. They were slapping out tortillas as a glint of sunlight appeared on the eastern horizon behind the mountains.

The women had fled with their children and little more than the clothes on their backs. They didn't know where they would spend the following night, or where the next meal would come from. But they invited us—affluent strangers from a country that was sponsoring a war against them—to partake in their meager breakfast. They shared everything they had with us. Our communion of tortillas and coffee at dawn was a rare sacrament of generosity and trust.

SCRIPTURE

Then the word of the Lord came to [Elijah], saying, "Go now to Zarephath, which belongs to Sidon, and live there; for I have commanded a widow there to feed you."

So he set out and went to Zarephath. When he came to the gate of the town, a widow was there gathering sticks; he called to her and said, "Bring me a little water in a vessel, so that I may drink." As she was going to bring it, he called to her and said, "Bring me a morsel of bread in your hand."

But she said, "As the Lord your God lives, I have nothing baked, only a handful of meal in a jar, and a little oil in a jug; I am now gathering a couple of sticks, so that I may go home and prepare if for myself and my son, that we may eat it, and die."

Elijah said to her, "Do not be afraid; go and do as you have said; but first make me a little cake of it and bring it to me, and afterwards make something for yourself and your son. For thus says the Lord the God of Israel: The jar of meal will not be emptied and the jug of oil will not fail until the day that the Lord sends rain on the earth."

She went and did as Elijah said, so that she as well as he and her household ate for many days. The jar of meal was not emptied, neither did the jug of oil fail, according to the word of the Lord that he spoke by Elijah.

⇥ 1 Kings 17:8-16

Do not store up for yourselves treasures on earth, where moth and rust consume and where thieves break in and steal; but store up for yourselves treasures in heaven, where neither moth nor rust consumes and where thieves do not break in and steal. For where your treasure is, there your heart will be also....

No one can serve two masters; for a slave will either hate one and love the other, or be devoted to the one and despise the other. You cannot serve God and wealth.

Therefore I tell you, do not worry about your life, what you will eat or what you will drink, or about your body, what you will wear. Is not life more than food, and the body more than clothing? Look at the birds of the air; they neither sow nor reap nor gather into barns, and yet your heavenly Father feeds them. Are you not of more value than they?...Consider the lilies of the field, how they grow; they neither toil nor spin, yet I tell you, even Solomon in all his glory was not clothed like one of these....But strive first for the kingdom of God and its righteousness, and all these things will be given to you as well.

⇥ Matthew 6:19-21, 24-26, 28-29, 33

The one who sows sparingly will also reap sparingly, and the one who sows bountifully will also reap bountifully ....And God is able to provide you with every blessing in abundance, so that by always having enough of everything, you may share abundantly in every good work. As it is written,

"He scatters abroad, he gives to the poor;
   his righteousness endures forever."

He who supplies seed to the sower and bread for food will supply and multiply your seed for sowing and increase the harvest of your righteousness. You will be enriched in every way for your great generosity, which will produce thanksgiving to God.

→ 2 Corinthians 9:6, 8-11

REFLECTION

The story of the widow of Zarephath is among the most poignant in scripture. We meet her as she gathers sticks in a time of famine, likely a gaunt and stooped figure at the gate of the town. She is preparing to fire up the oven for her last meal.

But Elijah asks her to give him bread. And she responds— at great risk. How difficult it must have been for this loving mother to deny her son food. How long had she saved this last crumb until they could no longer bear not to eat? And how did she explain to her poor, hungry child that this stranger would eat before he did?

Despite her great fear, she trusts that God's promise will be fulfilled. She is not disappointed. The jar of meal never grows empty, and the oil never fails. Her trust enables God to perform the miracle, and her entire household eats for days. Her circumstances go from desperate to abundant because of her faith.

It is no coincidence that God chose this widow to teach us about generosity. Under standard economic assumptions in every age, widows are the least likely to be generous because their vulnerability is greatest. The Bible's "widows and orphans" today is rendered "feminization of poverty."

And yet, as I learned on that early morning in Nicaragua, it is often those with the least who are the most generous—and the most grateful. They seem to have learned—as did Ruth and Naomi—that at the heart of their survival is an abiding trust in

God and a deep devotion to one another. When one suffers, all suffer. When one is blessed, all are blessed.

What transformation our world would undergo if we took that as our guiding principle today. We find our only true security in our faithful connection with one another, within a commitment that the needs of all will be met. That principle seems utterly naive in a world driven by consumerism and greed, where people judge success by how much they have rather than by how much they give. Words such as *Permanent* and *Perpetual*, *Trust* and *Security* appear frequently in the names of our banks, lulling us into believing that our money offers stability and salvation.

Mark 12:41-44 records the story of the widow who placed two copper coins worth a penny into the treasury. And Jesus said of her, "Truly I tell you, this poor widow has put in more than all those who are contributing to the treasury. For all of them have contributed out of their abundance; but she out of her poverty has put in everything she had, all she had to live on." In our age of financial planning, stock certificates, and IRAS, it is difficult to hear the small voice of the widows calling us to trust in God's provision—almost impossible to hear that tiny clink of change in the treasury among the shuffle of big bucks.

Blake Byler-Ortman was a missionary in El Salvador when an earthquake struck that tiny country. The uprooted Salvadorans shared their beans and rice with Blake, while he contacted churches in the United States, asking for clothing and medical supplies. Donations flooded in. Later, while reading Matthew 25, Blake reflected that if Jesus were to return today, people would probably get in the wrong lines. The Salvadorans, thinking they had shared nothing more than some beans and rice, would line up with the goats. And the U.S. Christians, who had sent boxes of supplies, would assume that they belonged with the sheep.

But those of us who are so terribly affluent by the world's standards must face some difficult truths. Two-thirds of the world's population is hungry. Every thirteen seconds a child dies of hunger on this globe that has enough to feed everyone, if we saw to it that what we have is shared. The middle and upper classes of the United States comprise about six percent of the global population but consume almost forty percent of the world's resources.

The truth behind the statistics came home to me when I lived with a group of students in New York City's East Harlem. A pastor there invited us to put ourselves in the following scene:

> You've been shipwrecked on an island with nine other people. Your food will last for several days, if among the ten of you, you eat only ten pieces of bread a day. Who among you would decide to eat six pieces of bread, leaving the other nine people to share four? Who would continue the practice, if you had to watch others die from starvation? That's the truth of living in a world where some of us use more than six times our share.

We so easily lose perspective on the fact that we live on an island of affluence in a starving world. We seem far from horrified at the glut of fast-food restaurants, shopping malls, luxury resorts, and car dealerships that consume our land and our souls. We so easily forget that our consumer goods often come to us at the price of virtual slave labor in Third World countries; that the bananas, pineapples, and hamburgers that grace our tables are grown or grazed on land that once belonged to simple farmers who fed their families, now taken over by U.S.-based multinational corporations to support our outrageous standard of living.

Jesus' words about simplicity and trust are perhaps the greatest challenge to materially comfortable Christians. Too often we embody the truth from Harry Emerson Fosdick's great hymn "God of Grace and God of Glory": We find ourselves "rich in things and poor in soul." In our economic lives more than anywhere else, we are likely to listen to the voices of our culture rather than the witness of the gospel. And if confronted, we are most likely to respond defensively.

What does it mean to follow a man who ordered his followers "to take nothing for their journey except a staff; no bread, no bag, no money in their belts" (Mark 6:8)? How many of us are attempting an impossible compromise between God and money?

Witnesses to another reality surround us, if we open our eyes to see them. A wealthy Episcopal church in Beverly Hills, outside Los Angeles, had established a sister church relationship with a poor parish in El Salvador, where workers make only a few pennies a day. Over time, the wealthy church prayed for the poor church and sent money for projects there. But when the poor parishioners in El Salvador heard that an earthquake had hit Los Angeles, they passed a hat during a worship service. They had known that form of devastation themselves. They collected a pile of coins equaling almost a thousand U.S. dollars for their sister church.

Several years ago, when an earthquake devastated Mexico, Christians in Nicaragua—who were suffering under a war at the time—organized a blood drive. They sent hundreds of pints of blood to the suffering people of Mexico with this message: "We have no money. We can only send our blood."

Earthquakes apparently move more than earth. They have moved hearts to sacrificial generosity, to levels that seem far beyond the means of those who are giving. As Paul wrote of the church in Macedonia,

> During a severe ordeal of affliction, their abundant joy and their extreme poverty have overflowed in a wealth of generosity on their part. For, as I can testify, they voluntarily gave according to their means, and even beyond their means (2 Cor. 8:2-3).

Jesus declared that the widow at the treasury gave "all that she had"—as we are called to give our whole selves to God, holding nothing back. That is the widows' invitation—to trust God in all things: with our fears and our doubts, our sorrows and our hopes, our sins and our strengths. Today we need to listen to the small voice of the widows who encourage us to care for one another and trust, for we are all bound to one another.

The echoes of a woman making bread for a prophet in ancient Israel rebounded across the globe centuries later in tortillas being slapped out at dawn in Nicaragua. They come to our ears today as an invitation to sacrificial generosity and radical trust in a God who provides for our needs—all our needs.

The widow of Zarephath gave everything—right down to the last crumb. And great was her reward. Each morning she went back to the jar of meal and found more. Each day she went to the bottle of oil and found plenty—because she loved God and trusted in God's provision. She learned the old truth: In love and resources, the more you give away, the more you have. The reality defies the laws of mathematics, but it's true. The more you trust, the more others will trust you; the more you know your need for God, the more God meets your need; the more grateful you are, the more you will have for which to be grateful.

The widows invite us to give all that we have—and all that we are—to God, who demands nothing less. We can rest secure in knowing that as we do so, the abundance that will return to us will be beyond measure.

FOR PRAYER AND DISCUSSION

1. What areas of my life bear evidence of my trust in God rather than in possessions or financial stability?

2. In what areas have I been generous?

3. What changes can I make that will enable me to live a life of more radical simplicity and generosity?

Gratitude

Like a Watered Garden

IN OCTOBER OF 1974, I RECEIVED A CALL with the news that my grandfather had died. In the hours after the call, memories of him flooded over me. I remembered the boxes of treasures that he pulled out for me when I was a child—full of Indian arrowheads, relics of the Civil War, colorful marbles used for playing Chinese checkers, rings and cards for magic tricks, and old coins.

We took walks together, my grandfather and I. He taught me how to identify trees by their leaves and bark, where to look in the forest for the mitten-leaved sassafras with its sweet-smelling bark, and the myrrh with a halo of seeds and a root that tasted like licorice. As a very young child, I trudged with him through deep snow with pockets full of birdseed to place on a rock or in the hollow of a tree, doing our part to ensure that wild birds and small animals didn't starve in winter. Those days often brought the excitement of discovering a wild rabbit burrowed into the snow or the tracks of a deer.

Our treks were education for me but also spiritual journey. I never got over my awe at the variety of God's good creatures, the delicacy of the wildflowers, the beauty of the sturdy trees. My grandfather taught me the kind of appreciation and trust for the Creator that comes from reveling in the creation.

The last time I saw my grandfather, I had grasped his frail, blue-veined hand and told him I was waiting for him to get better, so we could walk together again. He smiled. But cancer had claimed his stamina, and his already thin frame was getting thinner. That exchange in a hospital intensive-care room turned out to be our good-bye.

When I got the news of his death at my college in Maine, I immediately got on a bus headed for Boston, where I planned to catch a flight home to Pennsylvania. I still remember the brightness of that day—the red and gold leaves on the trees and a hot, yellow sun suspended in a brilliant blue sky. Though the bus carried only three other passengers, it felt stuffy. I felt closed in, full of grief, faint. And totally alone.

About halfway through the three-hour trip, a large woman, wearing a long, red, knit stocking cap over a shock of bright white hair, got on the bus. With thirty-eight empty seats from which to choose, she gathered up her bundles, tottered down the aisle, and fell in a heap in the seat beside mine, exclaiming, "Praise God, what a beautiful day!" I tried to smile at her, wondering to myself if it would be impolite to change my seat and trying to figure out how I could get around her.

After a moment's pause, she reached over, took my hand, and, with her warm eyes gazing into mine, gently asked, "Why are you so sad?" I found myself telling this stranger all about my grandfather. She asked questions and listened. And finally she said, "You must have loved him very much. How good of God to give you such a gift!" And with her subtle persuasion, I found my grief changing to gratitude.

Sarah Libby was a devoted Christian and an equally devoted Red Sox fan, who lived in a small room in an old rooming house in the shadow of Boston's Fenway Park. As we pulled into Boston, she gathered up her belongings and headed toward the door. Taking each stair slowly, she descended to get off. At the last step, she looked back at me and called, "Read Psalm 90!" and then disappeared into the crowd. At that moment I began to believe in angels.

I had a Bible with me. I opened it to Psalm 90 and read, "Our years come to an end like a sigh. / The days of our life are seventy years, / or perhaps eighty, if we are strong" (vss. 9-10). I smiled and wondered if Sarah Libby had known that my grandfather had died the day before his eightieth birthday. But what affected me most profoundly was the psalm's opening affirmation of God's power and presence and its closing invitation to joy:

> Lord, you have been our dwelling place
>   in all generations.
> Before the mountains were brought forth,
>   or ever you had formed the earth and the world,
>   from everlasting to everlasting you are God.
>
> . . . .
> Satisfy us in the morning with your steadfast love,
>   so that we may rejoice and be glad all our days.
>
> ✣ Psalm 90:1-2, 14

I found solace in those words, trusting that my grandfather was in God's hands. But I also trusted that I was in God's hands; that this "dwelling place," this home, was for me as well. I sensed God's love reaching back through the generations and forward to the children yet to be; and at the same time it was all around me like a comforting embrace. On one of the darkest days of my life, I was drenched with joy.

SCRIPTURE

> Praise the Lord!
>   O give thanks to the Lord,
>   for he is good;
>   for his steadfast love endures forever.
> Who can utter the mighty doings of the Lord,
>   or declare all his praise?
> Happy are those who observe justice,
>   who do righteousness at all times.
>
> ✣ Psalm 106:1-3

[May you] be filled with the knowledge of God's will in all spiritual wisdom and understanding, so that you may lead lives worthy of the Lord, fully pleasing to him, as you bear fruit in every good work and as you grow in the knowledge of God. May you be made strong with all the strength that comes from his glorious power, and may you be prepared to endure everything with patience, while joyfully giving thanks to the Father, who has enabled you to share in the inheritance of the saints in the light. He has rescued us from the power of darkness and transferred us into the kingdom of his beloved Son, in whom we have redemption, the forgiveness of sins.

> ➔ Colossians 1:9-14

Rejoice always, pray without ceasing, give thanks in all circumstances; for this is the will of God in Christ Jesus for you.

> ➔ 1 Thessalonians 5:16-18

REFLECTION

While in Nicaragua, I attended a worship service one Sunday. A few survivors of a village that had been massacred by the contras were in attendance. During the time of prayer, one woman tearfully addressed God. Her husband and three of her four children had been brutally murdered. This was her prayer: "Thank you, God, for sparing my daughter."

In South Africa, Archbishop Desmond Tutu told me the story of the squatter camp of Mogopa. Its residents received word one evening that their tin and corrugated-iron shacks would be bulldozed in the morning, which often happened under apartheid. Tutu arrived to hold a prayer service that lasted through the night. As the community gathered together, relying on one another for strength, an elderly man offered this prayer: "Thank you, God, for loving us."

In Washington, D.C., fire consumed a tenement around the corner from where I lived, a result of landlord negligence. Naomi Scott, who was a member of a neighborhood Bible study in which

I also participated, was severely burned and spent six months in the hospital on two separate occasions. She had to have several fingers amputated, and for a while she hovered near death. When our Bible study group asked her about the horrible experience months later, she said only, "I just thank God that I can still play the piano." Such gratitude overwhelms me.

Intercession flows rather easily for me. Someone is always in need: a lonely friend or a sick neighbor, a personal tragedy nearby or a war or natural disaster far away. I am much more attuned to need than thanksgiving.

I believe it is a discipline to be grateful. As Mary Glover's food-line prayer always reminded me, it's a blessed thing to start the day thanking God simply for creating it and awakening us to enjoy it. Thankfulness for life itself is a good starting point for those of us who more easily see what's wrong with the world than what's right.

A peculiar truth of our society, which promises so much, is this: The more we feel we are owed, the less able we are to be grateful for what we have. Our consumer culture cultivates dissatisfaction, always prompting us to hunger for more. Gratitude for faith, family, and friendship often pales in the clutter of possessions and promises that surround us.

But only one promise in life is sure: the salvation of God. We have been rescued from the power of darkness and transferred into the kingdom of light. For people in many parts of the world, that is sufficient to make them grateful all their days.

On another evening when neighbors and I were gathered for Bible study, we were mourning the death of a teenager who had been stabbed to death on the street earlier that day. He had been active in afterschool programs at the Sojourners Neighborhood Center for many years until the deadly tentacles of the illegal drug trade got him in their grasp.

At the time, Washington, D.C., had the highest homicide rate in the nation, and our neighborhood the highest rate in the city. One of the Bible study participants asked sadly, "What does it mean to follow Jesus in the most murderous neighborhood in the most murderous city in the most murderous nation in the world?" We had no answer to his challenge; his words met with silence as each of us pondered them.

Leaving the center, we walked out into cold darkness. The streetlight out front had been out for weeks. One of the mothers complained that she had spoken, without results, to city authorities about it several times on the phone. She had explained the danger for her children to come out onto a dark street.

As she was speaking, another mother pointed high into the sky and exclaimed, "Look!" There, surrounding a full moon, was a beautiful, circular rainbow, likely the product of ice crystals in the air reflecting the moon's light. None of us had ever seen such a sight. We gasped at the unique magnificence of it. "Thank you, Jesus!" the first mother shouted. *Sometimes*, I thought, *you need the darkness to see the light*.

Perhaps that's why people who endure great illness or even face death become more attuned to the blessings that surround them. Prayer usually becomes richer in times of crisis. Petitions are more numerous, but often so is thanksgiving. We have no right to ask for more if we are not first thankful for what we have been given.

Gratitude has the power to transform our relationship with God. In Isaiah's metaphor, God supplies all our needs. Like the rain that waters the earth, blessings continue to shower down upon us. We are the garden—urged to bloom and bear fruit in gratitude to the One who so gently tends and nurtures us. The fruits of our living are our thanksgiving to a generous God.

FOR PRAYER AND DISCUSSION

1. For what am I thankful?

2. What gets in the way of my being grateful?

3. What would it mean for me to live a life in praise of God, giving thanks in all circumstances?

Perseverance

A Spring Whose Waters Never Fail

IN NOVEMBER 1978, A MASSIVE STROKE claimed the speech and crippled the right side of Art Brown, my favorite college professor. Art had been a teacher, mentor, and friend. Four and a half years before, he had taken twenty other college students and me to East Harlem for six weeks, an experience that changed my life. I had always believed that, through the years, Art and I would continue to meet from time to time and carry on the theological and political conversation we had begun that spring in New York City.

But helpless tears—from both of us—marked my first visit after the stroke. The anguish was profound as Art started over again like a child, learning to speak, practicing simple arithmetic in his diary, and wrestling with emotions that often seemed out of control. His sentences often dangled in midair, unfinished.

Before leaving, I held his hand and offered a prayer. After my "Amen," Art began reciting the Lord's Prayer; it was the only thing his battered brain remembered from beginning to end. When he finished, he wept and said, "All I have left is faith. I cry to God that I can live a righteous life."

A year later, Art invited me to read his now-copious journals. I pored over them late into the night. On one page he pleaded, "Plug up the holes in my brain, please....They're killing me....They're making an awful draft." But an entry months later stated, "What a treasure trove I have stored up in my smashed brain." He was right. Where intellect had died, wit, warmth, and poetry had burst forth.

Of his struggle to speak, Art wrote, "As the voice of the female cricket speaks, so speak I unto thee, O Lord, for the female cricket makes no sound when it speaks." He reflected on his suffering, "A snowflake is a tiny thing compared to the sky. Pain is as nothing when measured to the tune of everything else in the universe."

Art's journals contained his reflections on whales and cobwebs, on unicorns and solar eclipses. He observed that "it's unfair to children to call owls wise." And he announced, "I want to spend the rest of my life playing 'Follow the Leader' with Christ."

I saw hope in Art's sense of humor, his ability to laugh at himself and his predicament, what he called "struggling from tears to cheers." He wrote about "mailslotitis," his inability to mail a letter without use of his right hand to hold the slot open. Reflecting after an operation, when to laugh pulled at his stitches and caused pain, he wrote, "If you can't laugh, be one." And of his dramatically changed life he asked, "Who am I? Who am I? Who am I? I really don't know the answer to all three of those questions."

Art's brain put forth remarkable puns and plays on words. On a hopeful day he recorded, "The worst of my stroke of bad luck is over." And on a sadder day, he wrote, "Pealing bells and peeling onions are not the same thing at all. But both can make you weep. Take away our crying and you deprive us of our humanity." Later he penned, "Tears are the telescope through which sometimes we see God."

On a later visit near Christmas, Art was showing me his art work. "Look at this one," he said as he held up a drawing labeled, "Hey, lady, you got eggs in a nest growing in your hair, in case you haven't noticed!" He explained that his unwieldy left hand had gotten a bit carried away with her bouffant hairstyle, and he had added the nest to justify all the extra hair.

Then he produced a large piece of white paper. On it he had drawn a small face surrounded by bold red strokes that swept in two large arcs toward the top of the page. The words he had crayoned at the bottom of the page read, "The late, great Aunt Minnie encased in a lobster claw." When I asked Art to explain, he grinned and said, "Well, I was trying to draw a Christmas angel—but it didn't come out quite right."

SCRIPTURE

Therefore, since we are justified by faith, we have peace with God through our Lord Jesus Christ, through whom we have obtained access to this grace in which we stand; and we boast in our hope of sharing the glory of God. And not only that, but we also boast in our sufferings, knowing that suffering produces endurance, and endurance produces character, and character produces hope, and hope does not disappoint us, because God's love has been poured into our hearts through the Holy Spirit that has been given to us....

For in hope we were saved. Now hope that is seen is not hope. For who hopes for what is seen? But if we hope for what we do not see, we wait for it with patience.

Likewise the Spirit helps us in our weakness; for we do not know how to pray as we ought, but that very Spirit intercedes with sighs too deep for words. And God, who searches the heart, knows what is the mind of the Spirit, because the Spirit intercedes for the saints according to the will of God.

We know that all things work together for good for those who love God, who are called according to his purpose.

↠ Romans 5:1-5; 8:24-28

We have this treasure in clay jars, so that it may be made clear that this extraordinary power belongs to God and does not come from us. We are afflicted in every way, but not crushed; perplexed, but not driven to despair; persecuted, but not forsaken; struck down, but not destroyed; always carrying in the body the death of Jesus, so that the life of Jesus may also be made visible in our bodies.

⇥ 2 Corinthians 4:7-10

Now faith is the assurance of things hoped for, the conviction of things not seen....

By faith Abraham obeyed when he was called to set out for a place that he was to receive as an inheritance;...By faith he received power of procreation, even though he was too old—and Sarah herself was barren—because he considered him faithful who had promised. By faith Moses was hidden by his parents for three months after his birth, because they saw that the child was beautiful and they were not afraid of the king's edict....By faith the people passed through the Red Sea as if it were dry land,...By faith Rahab the prostitute did not perish with those who were disobedient, because she had received the spies in peace....

Women received their dead by resurrection. Others were tortured, refusing to accept release, in order to obtain a better resurrection. Others suffered mocking and flogging, and even chains and imprisonment. They were stoned to death, they were sawn in two, they were killed by the sword; they went about in the skins of sheep and goats, destitute, persecuted, tormented—of whom the world was not worthy. They wandered in deserts and mountains, and in caves and holes in the ground.

Yet all these, though they were commended for their faith, did not receive what was promised, since God had provided something better so that they would not, apart from us, be made perfect.

Therefore, since we are surrounded by so great a cloud of witnesses, let us also lay aside every weight and the sin that clings so closely, and let us run with perseverance the race that is set before us, looking to Jesus the pioneer and perfecter of our faith, who for the sake of the joy that was set before him endured the cross, disregarding its shame, and has taken his seat at the right hand of the throne of God.

> → Hebrews 11:1, 8, 11, 23, 29, 31, 35–12:2

REFLECTION

The Hebrews passage is a sort of "roll call of faith." The passage lists the men and women—some named and some not—who went before us and blazed a trail of faithfulness. It's rather disturbing to read that most of them "did not receive what was promised." Most of them would not be regarded as great successes by anyone's standards.

I thought of them on a sweltering day in June 1984. With about fifty others, I was participating in a vigil for peace in downtown Washington. We were hoping to draw attention to a special government train that was carrying nuclear warheads throughout the United States—until recently, undetected. Our message depended on the media's paying some attention. But by midafternoon—long after the children's wagon-and-bicycle "peace train" had turned into a string of wilted streamers and popped balloons, and well into the day's worst heat—we ended our witness with a prayer, accepting that it had received little notice.

Five of us did make the local TV news that evening, however. After our tiring ordeal, we had made our way to the city's Rock Creek Park, where we plunged hot and exhausted into the cool water of the park's waterfall. We—along with a Salvadoran refugee family who joined us—became the focus of the annual first-hot-day-of-the-year human interest story on Channel 4, called "Washingtonians Beat the Heat"!

Things don't always go the way we plan or hope. But God calls us to faithfulness in spite of our failures and disappointments.

Several years ago, members of the tenants' union that Sojourners Community helped create went to a city council meeting to make a statement. A debate was taking place about rent control. I drove several neighbors, with their suitcases, downtown. They were going to the meeting to make the point that if rent control didn't pass in Washington, they would have to pack their bags and move out. It was a creative and courageous witness. But after the hearing, we learned that the city council had voted against us.

As we were returning to the neighborhood, I asked one woman if she felt disappointed. "No," she said confidently. "We'll get it next time." Another joined in, "The Bible says, 'It came to pass'; it doesn't say 'It came to stay.'"

I REMEMBER THAT STORY WHEN I NEED ENCOURAGEMENT. I consider those women part of the "cloud of witnesses" that keeps me going.

None of us can be strong all the time. Scripture reminds us that sometimes we're so weak the Spirit needs to intercede on our behalf. Sometimes we don't know what to pray—or how. Doubt, pain, confusion, shame—all are part of what it means to be human. But at our lowest points, we can trust that our rescue will come through "sighs too deep for words." Then our weakness reminds us that God's power—not our own—is at work in us. We cannot rescue ourselves.

All things work together for good, even if we can't see how at any particular moment. We are invited to trust in the spring whose waters never fail, in the boundless love of God. Our forebears faced the most brutal persecutions and remained faithful. They helped one another through the rough times, living as witnesses to faith for one another.

Hebrews reminds us that, though we may never see the hoped-for results, our disappointment simply puts us in good company. But most important of all, it notifies each of us of our responsibility to carry on—because "apart from us they should not be made perfect." We go on in faith for the sake of the faithful ones who went before us, trusting that we would follow—and for those who will come after us.

Penny Lernoux was a journalist whose life and faith dramatically changed through her personal witness of Latin American Christians' courageous struggle for justice. In the closing words of the last book she completed before her death, Lernoux quoted a young Guatemalan peasant woman, who herself was killed a few months later by Guatemalan soldiers. "What good is life," she said, "unless you give it away?—unless you can give it for a better world, even if you never see that world but have only carried your grain of sand to the building site. Then you're fulfilled as a person."

Historian Vincent Harding has said, "Living in faith is knowing that even though our little work, our little seed, our little brick may not make the whole thing, the whole thing exists in the mind of God, and that whether or not we are there to see the whole thing is not the most important matter. The most important thing is whether we have entered the process."

Harding likens the cloud of witnesses from Hebrews to "a great cheering squad for us. In the midst of everything that seems so difficult, that seems so powerful, that seems so overwhelming, they are saying to us: 'We are with you,' and 'There is a way through; there is a way to stand; there is a way to move; there is a way to hope; there is a way to believe. Don't give up!"

Our forebears in the faith have already faced everything that we are likely to face—and worse. And they issue an invitation for us to remain faithful, to meet them someday at the kingdom table to share a banquet of joy. Harding describes the scene:

Well, here we are, all present and accounted for. What a gang! What a table! What a host! What a chance for holding and being held, for feeding and being fed, for giving, receiving, and being the light.

No excuse for drooping—at least not for long. No excuse for not running—or at least walking strong. No excuse for staying down. 'Cause we are surrounded, folks. So, let's straighten up; let's get refreshed at the table, and then get down with some real long-distance walking and running—and maybe even some flying, like eagles, in due time. That's our tradition. That's our destiny. That's our hope. So go right on, sisters and brothers, people of the tents: walk in the light, run with the cloud, mount up on wings, follow the Pioneer. There is a city to build.

Art Brown is part of that great cloud of witnesses. I thank God for him and all the others who have surrounded me with hope. In the years before his death, he taught me what it means to persevere. Faith and humor are necessary ingredients. I know now that that lesson is more important than all I could have gleaned from him in a lifetime of theological conversations.

I never saw such a longing in anyone—so evident in Art's eyes—for God, for healing, for understanding; above all, for God. When all else is stripped away, faith remains. Art learned childlike faith and total dependence on God and invites us to the same. He invites us all to spend the rest of our lives playing follow the leader with Jesus. It's an admirable vocation.

Art served as a reminder that as we try to follow, we won't always be graceful or articulate or successful. But with a grain of faith and a dose of humor, we can learn to go on with what we are given. And if a Christmas angel looks more like Aunt Minnie in the clutches of a killer lobster, so be it.

FOR PRAYER AND DISCUSSION

1. When has my suffering drawn me closer to God?

2. When has tragedy or disappointment caused me to lose faith? How did I return to hope and to God?

3. How can my pain deepen and enrich my intercession for others who suffer?

Solidarity

Raise Up the Foundations

EVERAL YEARS AGO, WHILE AT A CONFERENCE in Tucson, Arizona, I met some members of a Christian base community in Mexico. They drew inspiration for their shared life from regular reflection on scripture and encouragement from the witness of other Christian base communities throughout Latin America. They related the following story to me: In an isolated rural area of Brazil, members of a small base community were locked in a battle for survival. Just as they prepared to harvest their crops, the Brazilian parliament voted to take over their land for a government project. The community moved on and planted again. Once again a vote of parliament pushed them off their land before they could harvest.

When parliament threatened a third time, the community members grew desperate. Their children were hungry. They knew that to move on would mean death by starvation for them. But to stay would likely mean death by government forces for the entire community. An emotional discussion took place. Finally a woman rose and said she had a plan.

A few days later, the woman appeared in a wealthy suburb of a city that was a long walk from her home. She and her ragged children sat down on the beautiful lawn in front of the house of a parliament member. Soon a servant came out and offered them bread. But the woman refused it. "We have not come for bread," she said, and the servant went back to the house. Before long, he returned with a handful of money. "We do not want your money," the mother said.

Baffled, the wife of the parliament member, who had been watching from inside, eventually came out. "What do you want?" she asked the poor woman.

"We're going to die," she replied. "And this is such a nice place, we thought we'd die here."

"But why are you going to die?" the stunned wife asked. The woman explained what was happening to her community. Similar conversations were taking place in all the wealthy parts of the city, where other community mothers had gone with their children.

Soon the phones were ringing off the hook at the parliament. Each wife was so moved that she called her husband to tell the story. The vote never took place, and the community members harvested their crops in peace.

SCRIPTURE

Awe came upon everyone, because many wonders and signs were being done by the apostles....Day by day, as they spent much time together in the temple, they broke bread at home and ate their food with glad and generous hearts, praising God and having the goodwill of all the people. And day by day the Lord added to their number those who were being saved....

Now the whole group of those who believed were of one heart and soul, and no one claimed private ownership of any possessions, but everything they owned was held in common. With great power the apostles gave their testimony to the resurrection of the Lord Jesus, and great grace was upon them all. There was not a needy person among them, for as many as owned lands or houses sold them and brought the proceeds of what was sold. They laid it at the apostles' feet, and it was distributed to each as any had need.

→ Acts 2:43, 46-47; 4:32-35

Let love be genuine; hate what is evil, hold fast to what is good; love one another with mutual affection; outdo one another in showing honor. Do not lag in zeal, be ardent in spirit, serve the Lord. Rejoice in hope, be patient in suffering, persevere in prayer. Contribute to the needs of the saints; extend hospitality to strangers.

Bless those who persecute you; bless and do not curse them. Rejoice with those who rejoice, weep with those who weep. Live in harmony with one another; do not be haughty, but associate with the lowly; do not claim to be wiser than you are. Do not repay anyone evil for evil, but take thought for what is noble in the sight of all. If it is possible, so far as it depends on you, live peaceably with all. Beloved, never avenge yourselves, but leave room for the wrath of God....No, "if your enemies are hungry, feed them; if they are thirsty, give them something to drink; for by doing this you will heap burning coals on their heads." Do not be overcome by evil, but overcome evil with good.

⤳ Romans 12:9-21

As God's chosen ones, holy and beloved, clothe yourselves with compassion, kindness, humility, meekness, and patience. Bear with one another and, if anyone has a complaint against another, forgive each other; just as the Lord has forgiven you, so you also must forgive. Above all, clothe yourselves with love, which binds everything together in perfect harmony. And let the peace of Christ rule in your hearts, to which indeed you were called in the one body. And be thankful. Let the word of Christ dwell in you richly; teach and admonish one another in all wisdom; and with gratitude in your hearts sing psalms, hymns, and spiritual songs to God. And whatever you do, in word or deed, do everything in the name of the Lord Jesus, giving thanks to God the Father through him.

⤳ Colossians 3:12-17

REFLECTION

It wasn't a plan or a strategy. No one had a blueprint. It's simply what happened when the Spirit rushed upon the members of the early church. In the heady aftermath of Pentecost, believers began to share all that they had, and the church started to look like a family. No one claimed ownership of anything, and everyone's needs were met.

To live like that in the twentieth century is enough to get you labeled a communist. The modern gospel of prosperity, which equates wealth and security with the Spirit's rewards, is a far cry from the radical ways of the early Jerusalem church—as are the competition and individualism that mark life in our society and many others.

People came in droves to join the early Christians, but attendance is down in U.S. churches. The life of believers then was a stark contrast to the culture around them. They lived simply, with glad and generous hearts. They enjoyed one another's hospitality and knew their financial security rested on their trust in God and their bonds with one another. They shone like a light.

Christian communities of a similar sort thrive today in parts of the world that are marked by poverty, violence, and oppression. In those places, people seem to know their need for God and one another, and they rely on interdependence for security. In the 1970s and 1980s, in war-torn Latin America and the poorest parts of Asia and Africa, the Christian base community movement flourished. Persecution only seemed to deepen the bonds, as it did among the earliest believers.

Often in these places, Christians were accused of being communists. Repressive governments reacted with torture and violence to organized efforts for fair wages and equal land distribution—and to demands that the benefits of the land rightfully belonged to indigenous people and not U.S. corporations.

The inspiration for the actions of these Christian communities came not primarily from political ideals but from the promises of the Bible. When Christians in these countries read about the rich being dethroned and the poor being exalted, they believed it. When they saw themselves as the hungry who were promised food, they went into action.

The members of the Brazilian base community understood that either they lived together, or they died together. The fate of one was the fate of all. Their solidarity with one another built a strong foundation that drew the compassionate wives of parliament members into the circle. That solidarity is perhaps best summed up in Romans 12:15, "Rejoice with those who rejoice, weep with those who weep."

Life-and-death situations here often have the same effect of drawing people together into remarkable solidarity. When we learn that a friend or church member has lost a loved one or been diagnosed with a serious illness, we usually are quick to share the burden. Most crises bring a flood of prayers, cards, flowers, and food from a wide and caring circle.

When I worked as a chaplain on the cancer ward of a children's hospital in Atlanta, I watched patients grieve over changes in their appearance. One twelve year old with leukemia, who was undergoing chemotherapy, cried every time she brushed her hair. She soon began collecting it as it fell out and kept it in a plastic bag on her dresser.

Every time I observed such anguish, I recalled a story told by Fred Craddock: An eleven-year-old boy was recovering from cancer and the devastating effects of chemotherapy. When it came time for him to return to school, he and his parents experimented with hats, wigs, and bandannas in an attempt to conceal his baldness. They finally settled on a baseball cap, but the boy still feared the taunts he would receive for looking "different." Mustering up his courage, he went to school wearing his cap—only to discover that all of his friends had shaved their heads.

We can't hide the pain of the world. We can't cover it up. We can only share it—and make someone else's journey a little easier. That classroom of eleven year olds understood solidarity.

It's usually easier to respond to a short-term crisis; it's much more difficult to build solidarity with one another over the long haul, to live each day as if our lives depended on one another. My two decades of involvement with intentional Christian communities have taught me that building community requires great effort in this society.

We find it difficult to trust, to unlearn the ways of private ownership and personal control and prideful competition. The challenges of sharing space and economic resources have taught me how much I still need conversion to the way of Christ. And I have come to know deeply the power of confession and forgiveness, requirements for building a life together.

Dr. David Hilfiker is one of the founders of Joseph's House, a community comprised of medical personnel and formerly homeless men with AIDS in Washington, D.C. The house abounds with "resurrection" stories: remarkable turn-arounds in the lives of men who were left to die on the streets but who have healed and flourished in the house's caring environment. Hilfiker says,

> The issue with middle-class Americans is our unwillingness—and the impropriety—of exposing our weakness and vulnerability.
>
> We are supposed to be independent, to take care of ourselves. Healing means beginning to see our own [weakness and sin]. One thing that is so therapeutic [at Joseph's House] for me is to see my own weakness and vulnerability so honored and accepted. The men all know what it's like not to be doing well.

Dr. Hilfiker goes on to state that AIDS was a wake-up call for most of the men, a "death sentence" that ironically ended up saving their lives by forcing changes in behavior. "Chances are some of these men would be dead now if it weren't for the disease. It destroys the fantasy of our independence, which is a problem for all of us. When we get rid of the fantasy, it allows for community."

To live closely bound to one another presents great challenges. But despite the difficulties, we are called to be the body of Christ. We are commanded to strive toward harmony and be committed to one another in love—indeed, to be willing to lay down our lives for one another (John 15:13). This is part of the spiritual richness of the Christian life.

Isaiah 5:8 describes the sad alternative: "Ah, you who join house to house, who add field to field, until there is room for no one but you, and you are left to live alone in the midst of the land!" Accumulation is the antithesis of community.

The sixth-century monk Dorotheus of Gaza imagined the world as a large circle with God at the middle. In his picture, we human beings start our lives at the circle's edge. As we grow closer to God, journeying toward the center of the circle, we also move closer to one another. Such is the truth of solidarity.

Our model is no less than God. Incarnation was God's choice to come to earth and share our pain and our joys, to know our sorrows and our hopes. On the cross, Jesus made the ultimate gesture of solidarity, taking upon himself our sins and sufferings.

Jesus' prayer in the moments before the arrest that led to his death was for the unity of his followers. He prayed to God for his disciples and all believers to come:

> As you, Father, are in me and I am in you, may they also be in us....The glory that you have given me I have given them, so that they may be one, as we are one, I in them and you in me, that they may become completely one, so that the world may know that you have sent me and have loved them even as you have loved me (John 17:21-23).

The wish of a man facing death was that we honor his life and his death by living in solidarity with him, with God, and with one another. In so doing, we proclaim to the world that the promises of Jesus can be trusted.

FOR PRAYER AND DISCUSSION

1. Where in my life do I experience community with other believers?

2. How can my prayers be a means of increasing my solidarity with others?

3. How can I experience more of the generosity, gladness, and hospitality that marked the early church?

Reconciliation

Repairer of the Breach

JUBILEE PARTNERS IN RURAL COMER, GEORGIA, is a Christian community that ministers to refugees. In its almost two decades of existence, the community has welcomed people from areas of war and famine all over the globe: Cambodia, Cuba, El Salvador, Vietnam, Nicaragua, Afghanistan, Haiti, Guatemala, Bosnia. Many arrive traumatized and fearful from their recent experiences.

One cool evening in the fall of 1994, recently arrived Bosnian refugees gathered around a bonfire and tearfully shared songs from their homeland. After the singing, a Muslim man said, "I don't understand what happened. For years we were neighbors, often best friends. Then, this demonic force called 'ethnic cleansing' broke out among us—and now we are killing each other on sight."

At the time, vengeful preelection rhetoric was rampant in this country, as politicians tried to outdo one another in getting "tough on crime." In response, twenty-five members of a group called Murder Victims' Families for Reconciliation drove across Georgia in a bus, telling their stories. They called it a Journey of Hope. All had experienced the murder of a loved one. And all had taken the long journey from grief through hatred and bitterness to forgiveness.

Jubilee Partners hosted the group one evening, and George

White told his story. George's wife had been murdered in southern Alabama. George had been wounded by the gunman, but he was convicted of the murder. He spent several years in prison before he was able to prove his innocence. During that time his teenage children helped him overcome the hatred he felt toward the killer and all those who had participated in the gross miscarriage of justice that almost destroyed his life.

As George told his story, a sixteen-year-old Bosnian, who was just beginning to learn English, struggled to follow along. When he finished, Don Mosley, a founder of the community, leaned over and asked her if she understood George's words.

"Yes," she replied. "I understand—but I don't understand. A man kill your wife, and you forgive that man? I don't understand how it is possible!" Her eyes brimmed with tears as she stood up and said haltingly, "I hope I can forgive the Serbs like that in ten years."

George White, whose daughter was just about her age, crossed the room, gently placed his hands on her shoulders, and said, "You have to try. It's the only way to heal from this mess."

SCRIPTURE

[Jesus] left Judea and started back to Galilee. But he had to go through Samaria. So he came to a Samaritan city called Sychar, near the plot of ground that Jacob had given to his son Joseph. Jacob's well was there, and Jesus, tired out by his journey, was sitting by the well. It was about noon.

A Samaritan woman came to draw water, and Jesus said to her, "Give me a drink."...The Samaritan woman said to him, "How is it that you, a Jew, ask a drink of me, a woman of Samaria?" (Jews do not share things in common with Samaritans.)...

Jesus said to her, "Everyone who drinks of this water will be thirsty again, but those who drink of the water that I will give them will never be thirsty. The water that I will give will become in them a spring of water gushing up to eternal life." The woman said to him, "Sir, give me this water, so that I may never be thirsty or have to keep coming here to draw water."

Jesus said to her, "Go, call your husband, and come back." The woman answered him, "I have no husband." Jesus said to her, "You are right in saying, 'I have no husband'; for you have had five husbands, and the one you have now is not your husband. What you have said is true!"

The woman said to him, "Sir, I see that you are a prophet. Our ancestors worshiped on this mountain, but you say that the place where people must worship is in Jerusalem." Jesus said to her, "Woman, believe me...the hour is coming and is now here, when the true worshipers will worship the Father in spirit and truth."...

The woman said to him, "I know that Messiah is coming....When he comes, he will proclaim all things to us." Jesus said to her, "I am he, the one who is speaking to you."

Just then the disciples came. They were astonished that he was speaking with a woman....Then the woman left her water jar and went back to the city....Many Samaritans from that city believed in him because of the woman's testimony.

↝ John 4:3-28, 39

From now on, therefore, we regard no one from a human point of view; even though we once knew Christ from a human point of view, we know him no longer in that way. So if anyone is in Christ, there is a new creation; everything old has passed away; see, everything has become new! All this is from God, who reconciled us to himself through Christ, and has given us the ministry of reconciliation.

↝ 2 Corinthians 5:16-18

But now in Christ Jesus you who once were far off have been brought near by the blood of Christ. For he is our peace; in his flesh he has made both groups into one and has broken down the dividing wall, that is, the hostility between us...that he might create in himself one new humanity in place of the two, thus making peace, and might reconcile both groups to God in one body, through the cross, thus putting to death that hostility through it. So he came and proclaimed peace to you who were far off and peace to those who were near; for through him both of us have access in one Spirit to [God].....in [Christ] you are built together spiritually into a dwelling place for God.

→ Ephesians 2:13-18, 22

REFLECTION

The "woman at the well" is one of the few women I remember being pictured in our Sunday school material when I was a child. She carried a large blue water jar on her shoulder, which she left by the well when she ran to tell the townspeople about "living water." But much of the story's impact escaped me when I was young. I didn't realize what a scandal it was that Jesus was talking with her.

Jews and Samaritans were mortal enemies. The Samaritans were a mixed race, considered by the Jews to be impure and inferior, religious apostates. It was no coincidence that Jesus told a parable about a wounded Jew at the side of the road being cared for by a Samaritan: He was broadening the definition of "neighbor," making a point about inclusiveness. To most Jews, the concept of a "good Samaritan" was an oxymoron. Samaritans and Jews didn't mingle; they didn't talk; and they certainly didn't share a drink of water. Thus the woman asked Jesus, "How is it that you, a Jew, ask a drink of me, a woman of Samaria?"

Beyond the issue of race, the woman also questioned the gesture because she was female. In that time, Jewish men didn't speak to women in public. The Pharisees, who made a career of following the letter of the law, would often walk into walls or other obstacles to avoid looking at a woman or talking with one. Women were considered second-class citizens and unreliable witnesses. No wonder, then, that the disciples were "astonished" to find Jesus speaking with this woman.

One other detail to note is the time of day at which their conversation (the longest recorded between Jesus and anyone) took place. Most water gatherers met at wells in the early morning or at dusk—away from the intense heat of the midday. But Jesus and the woman met about noon. Maybe she was trying to avoid contact and conversation with the other women of Sychar. Perhaps her history made her an object of their gossip and scorn. After all, she had had five husbands, and she was not married to the man with whom she was living at the time. To have been cast aside by so many men and to be unmarried rendered her financially insecure.

Add all this together, and she might well be regarded as the "ultimate outcast": a woman, a foreigner, an enemy, a sinner, and poor. In one trip to the enemy territory of Samaria, in one conversation, Jesus crossed the great divides of race, gender, and social location. That Jesus chose this most unlikely of candidates, this most unbelievable of persons to reveal that he was the Messiah is truly astounding.

According to Ephesians, through the cross Jesus broke down the "dividing walls" within humanity. In Jesus' day, the great division was between Jew and Gentile. Today, we experience division along lines of race, gender, age, and ability, to name just a few of the walls among us. But perhaps the most obvious division is economic. A U.S. census report released in the summer of 1996 declared that the gap between rich and poor in this country is the greatest it has been in fifty years; the nation is more economically polarized than at any time since the end of World War II.

The richest one percent of Americans now own forty-two percent of the national wealth; the top tenth control eighty percent. It is not simply the poor who are being left out as more and more wealth is being concentrated in the hands of an elite few. Such disparity undermines democracy; raises the insecurity of the middle class; and renders food, shelter, employment, medical care, and education—all basic rights in an equitable society—as commodities beyond the reach of more and more citizens. Attaining a "stable" economic life requires increasing investments of time and energy, leading to a disintegration in family life and spiritual growth.

The concentration of wealth in this country makes us all more vulnerable; and in truth, we have much more in common with the poor than we would like to admit. Too many people give in to the lie that it is the lower classes and refugees who threaten our stability as a nation, when actually the opposite is true. We have created all sorts of places to separate and hide the poor: cells and camps, ghettos and barrios, institutions and reservations. Yet of all the walls in the world, the most destructive is the one that goes through our hearts, the one that shuts out the world's suffering.

Inside government buildings in Washington, D.C., hands shape the policies that run the world; outside, other hands rub themselves raw over steam grates trying to keep warm. Suburban white children learn on state-of-the-art computers, compete in after-school sports, and hope to get into the college of their choice; ethnic inner-city children pray not to get caught in gunfire. In the neighborhood where I lived for fifteen years, children as young as eight wear pagers, ready for a signal from a drug dealer to run drugs—their way of supporting their mothers and siblings. The breach we have created is massive.

Dr. Hilfiker of Joseph's House says that at one time if he advocated persistently enough, he could always get care for his patients, even the most indigent. The privatization of medical care and the entrepreneurial spirit that dominates the health care system have changed that:

> We are increasingly willing to ghettoize people into certain areas geographically and say, "I'm sorry, but we really can't take care of your problem." From a spiritual point of view, that destroys a nation.

Our reflection on this issue compels each of us to ask, What is the great divide for me today? Where is "Samaria," the enemy territory that I dare not risk entering? What barrier might I be urged to cross?

In the fall of 1981, congressional hearings took me to Washington, D.C.'s Capitol Hill. Colorful banners hung from all the upscale cafes and pubs: "Celebrate the New Year with us!" "Ring in the New Year here!" These messages were not particularly exceptional—except that this was the last weekend in September. Clarity came when I spied a sign that read, "Party here for the fiscal New Year!" The banners proclaimed the year determined by money, the one that begins on October 1.

A week later when the new fiscal year arrived, I was serving the first of five consecutive weekends in jail for an act of protest at the annual nuclear arms exposition. I talked with my cell mates over a meal that consisted of a glob of cold noodles with a congealed pile of bland yellow gravy.

The women were well aware that the new administration meant the shifting of budget priorities. They spoke fearfully of an end to educational and job-training opportunities, to medical services and drug rehabilitation programs. They wondered how they would pay their rent and feed their children. I hoped that they were overreacting; but as the 1980s progressed, their worst fears came true.

That weekend behind bars was an education in perspective: Whether or not the fiscal new year was something to celebrate depended on whether you were sitting in a Capitol Hill cafe or the D.C. jail.

A similar moment occurred a month later. I was staffing an overnight shelter at a local church. Sixty homeless men were asleep in the fellowship hall. A knock came at the church door at about three o'clock in the morning. I opened the door a crack to find two young Latinas on the stoop, clutching three babies and two garbage bags full of possessions. They told me in Spanish that the police had sent them; they needed a place to spend the night.

I tried to tell them there was no room. My Spanish was awkward. Their weary eyes pleaded for rest as a gust of bone-chilling air rushed in from outside where they stood. One by one the babies started to cry. I relented.

Three other children appeared from behind them as I ushered the small parade through the chorus of snores back to the kitchen, where I had hoped to get a few hours of sleep. I lifted my sleeping bag off the floor and spread it in the basket of the large dishwasher to make a bed for the six-month-old twins, then heated some milk for them. I went in search of blankets and returned with several. We found spaces between the cabinets, under the tables, in front of the refrigerators. All were soon sound asleep—all except one.

Four-year-old María climbed into my lap and whimpered softly as I stroked her hair. Sitting on a blanket on the concrete floor, I cradled and rocked her until she fell asleep. But a rush of images flooded my mind and kept me from nodding off.

On this late-October early morning, I pictured Halloweens gone by in my hometown of Hershey, Pennsylvania: shuffling with my sisters through fallen leaves in homemade costumes, past grinning jack-o'-lanterns on porches, returning home with grocery bags brimming with candy (mostly Hershey bars, of course). I remembered Christmas caroling on those same streets, being invited in by neighbors for a mug of steaming hot chocolate. I conjured pleasant memories of sledding in winter on the hilly street next to our house and playing on homemade stilts and skateboards in summer.

María stirred slightly, repositioning herself. Then she sighed heavily. And I wondered what it must be like to have a childhood without a home.

Many of us in U.S. churches are too well-educated and too well-loved to understand fully the desperation of poverty or homelessness. But we are invited and urged to try. We can cross the boundaries that separate us and learn what it means to make the struggles of the powerless and the desperate our own, as Jesus did. As one ancient Greek philosopher replied when asked when there would be justice, "Justice will come when those of us who are not injured are as indignant as those who are."

Isaiah reminds us that we are called to be "repairers of the breach" and "restorers of streets to live in." The massive societal breach in this country is an affront to God. So too are the streets that have become places of violent death rather than thriving life.

The temptation is always to believe that there is an "us" and a "them." But the truth is that we are all part of the human family. The objectification and sacrifice of the poor only dehumanizes and damages us all. If some are expendable, before long we will all be expendable.

We follow a savior who put an end to the vengeful "eye for an eye" response (Matt. 5:38-39). His command was clear: "But I say to you, Love your enemies and pray for those who persecute you" (Matt. 5:44). It is an astounding, impractical demand. It's so much easier to keep the "enemies" at arm's length.

I didn't really know what this verse meant for me until I began working as a court advocate for battered women in the mountains of western North Carolina a few years ago. On my most difficult day in court, the assistant district attorney cleared the courtroom before the hearing, hoping to avoid the possibility of violence. The defendant, my client's husband, was known to own thirteen guns. Two sheriff's deputies searched him twice.

During the proceedings I stood between the defendant and my client, who had suffered under a reign of terror and humiliation for thirteen years. Three days before, when her husband broke her cheekbone with a blow of his fist, she decided it was time to leave him. She got a restraining order for herself and her children. But, as she told me afterward, "It's only a piece of paper. It's not going to stop him if he really wants to hurt me again." She was right, of course.

Outside, her husband approached me in the parking lot. He began telling me of his own abuse as a child. His voice broke as he told me how hard it would be on him not to see his own children. He said he was sorry for the violence he had done; he wished he knew how to behave differently. That moment was a turning point for me. I soon began cofacilitating a weekly anger management group for men who batter.

One week I sat across from a man who had videotaped himself repeatedly raping his wife. He had beaten her one night, told her "Men beat their dogs," and then forced her to sleep out on the porch with the family pet. On another occasion, he had attempted to strangle her with the telephone cord when she tried to call for help. She finally appeared in court after he held a gun to her head through an entire night, threatening to kill her if she moved. In his presence, I felt a fear more intense than I had ever known.

I can't say that I learned to love these men, these "enemies." But I did take some steps toward understanding and caring for men who do violence. I consider it a privilege to have been allowed to know some of their fears and hopes. Somehow we are all entangled in this brokenness together, and we need to find our way out together.

Soon after I began my court advocacy work, I attended a church-sponsored conference on domestic violence. Many of those present were survivors of domestic or sexual abuse, and wounds were still raw. Anger was the prevailing emotion. Both survivors and justice advocates expressed the belief that forgiveness is naive and reconciliation impossible.

I have shared their rage and despair. I understand that such feelings are a natural reaction to being told, as most battered women are, that the first step in healing is to forgive. But I'm not yet ready to concede that we can't build a world in which reconciliation is possible without sacrificing justice. Forgiveness is certainly not the first step, but perhaps it could be the last.

George White learned that truth. He refused to accept the barriers set up between him and his wife's killer. He knew that mercy and compassion are the only way out of a world marked by vengeance and violence, whose escalation threatens to engulf us all. He tried another perspective and saw a glimpse of truth —a truth that remains elusive if we refuse to step beyond the boundaries prescribed for us by race and status; class, gender, and age.

Jesus invites us to see with his eyes—no longer with the judgment so natural for us human beings but with the love through which he views each one of us. He crossed boundaries, serving as a "repairer of the breach." He went to his death uttering the words, "Father, forgive them." His only vengeance was resurrection. And he has entrusted us to carry on the ministry of reconciliation that he began on the cross.

In a baptismal formula, the early church proclaimed,

In Christ Jesus you are all children of God through faith. As many of you as were baptized into Christ have clothed yourselves with Christ. There is no longer Jew or Greek, there is no longer slave or free, there is no longer male and female; for all of you are one in Christ Jesus" (Gal. 3:26-28).

Baptism into the Christian faith initiated a person into a radically new social order in which all participated equally and viewed others only from the perspective of the love of Christ. That all-inclusive love tore down the oppressive distinctions that had been used to oppress and separate. The invitation to the new social order still stands.

FOR PRAYER AND DISCUSSION

1. Into what "Samaria" might Jesus be inviting me?

2. What does it mean for me to be entrusted with the ministry of reconciliation?

3. How do I live out the truth of Galatians 3:26-28 in my faith life: "clothed with Christ" and dedicated to breaking down distinctions that keep people apart?

Joy

Gloom Be Like the Noonday

TRAGEDY MARKED THE DAYS preceding Christmas in a Honduran refugee camp filled with Salvadorans who had tried to flee the violence engulfing their country. National guard members had tracked down a young catechist, bound him by his thumbs, and taken him away. When he tried to escape, they mowed him down with machine-gun fire. Later his pregnant wife and five children gathered around his coffin as a single candle burned in the darkness.

In another part of the camp, a group of women surrounded an infant and sang to him in a dark tent, lit only by the light of a candle. Between the verses of the song, the anguished cries of his mother filled the air. She had fed her son through the night from an eyedropper, trying to coax some nourishment into his starving body.

The child lay in the center of them, his eyes and mouth open. He did not cry. One of the mothers marked the sign of the cross on the child's forehead while he looked at them fervently, as if expecting an answer to a question he could not ask. Then the singing stopped. The child was dead.

Despite such sorrow, when Christmas Eve came, the camp burst into joyful preparation. Women baked sweet cinnamon bread in an adobe oven, while men butchered hogs for the making of special pork tamales. The children made figurines out of

91

clay from the riverbed for the nativity scene, adding local touch-
es to the usual characters: pigs, an armadillo, and baby Jesus
sleeping in a hammock. They painted beans and kernels of corn
in bright colors and strung them into garlands. They made orna-
ments from small medicine boxes and shaped figures from the
tin foil that wraps margarine sticks and hung these on a tree
branch.

The children dressed as shepherds and passed from tent to
tent, recounting the journey of María and José in search of shelter. "This Christmas we will celebrate as they did," said one
mother, "looking for a place where our children can be born."

A refugee woman asked Yvonne Dilling, a U.S. church worker
from Indiana in the camp, why she always looked so sad and
burdened. Yvonne talked about the grief she felt over all the suffering she was witnessing and her commitment to give all of
herself to the refugees' struggle.

The woman gently confronted her: "Only people who expect
to go back to the United States in a year work the way you do.
You cannot be serious about our struggle unless you play and
celebrate and do those things that make it possible to give a lifetime to it."

She reminded Yvonne that every time the refugees were dis-
placed and had to build a new camp, they immediately formed
three committees: a construction committee, an education committee, and the *comité de alegría*—"the committee of joy." Celebration was as basic to the life of the refugees as digging latrines
and teaching their children to read.

SCRIPTURE

When the Lord restored the fortunes of Zion,
    we were like those who dream.
Then our mouth was filled with laughter,
    and our tongue with shouts of joy;
then it was said among the nations,
    "The Lord has done great things for them."

The Lord has done great things for us,
    and we rejoiced.

Restore our fortunes, O Lord,
    like the watercourses in the Negeb.
May those who sow in tears reap with shouts of joy.
Those who go out weeping,
    bearing the seed for sowing,
shall come home with shouts of joy,
    carrying their sheaves.

→ Psalm 126

Very truly, I tell you, you will weep and mourn, but the world will rejoice; you will have pain, but your pain will turn into joy. When a woman is in labor, she has pain, because her hour has come. But when her child is born, she no longer remembers the anguish because of the joy of having brought a human being into the world. So you have pain now; but I will see you again, and your hearts will rejoice, and no one will take your joy from you....Ask and you will receive, so that your joy may be complete.

→ John 16:20-22, 24

Rejoice in the Lord always; again I will say, Rejoice. Let your gentleness be known to everyone. The Lord is near. Do not worry about anything, but in everything in prayer and supplication with thanksgiving let your requests be made known to God. And the peace of God, which surpasses all understanding, will guard your hearts and your minds in Christ Jesus.

→ Philippians 4:4-7

REFLECTION

Just as people with the least are often the most grateful and generous, I have found that people who suffer most are often the most joyful—another irony of faithfulness. Their joy is something wholly other than the sort of shallow happiness that the world offers. It comes not from trying to avoid pain by accruing comforts but rather from moving deeply into the world's pain and finding reasons to rejoice in the midst of embracing what is difficult. It is the joy of resurrection, known only by passing through crucifixion.

During my first winter in Washington, D.C., I had to visit the public health clinic just before Christmas. Walking past piles of dirty gray snow, over sidewalks strewn with broken glass, I was despairing that the season fast approaching seemed so joyless in this desolate neighborhood.

At the clinic, I found the small waiting room packed with people—elderly folks, crying children, and mothers trying to pull mittens and boots off the crying ones. Cheap tinsel and Christmas greetings in crayoned cardboard letters decorated the walls. Someone had painted the face of the plastic Santa Claus on the file cabinet black. In the next room, a woman moaned about a piece of glass in her foot and pleaded with the doctor, "Please just amputate it"; across the hall a baby wailed.

I took a seat and asked the woman next to me how long she had been waiting. Two hours. The receptionist, a young woman, approached and handed me a pile of forms to fill out. Her eyes looked weary, and exhaustion marked her tone as she explained what I needed to do. I asked her where she was from.

"El Salvador," she said, allowing a smile to come to her face. She told me how much pain she felt being separated from her family—still in El Salvador—at Christmas. "But," she said, "every year I save up my money. If I save carefully, I can save thirty dollars to call home at Christmas. That's for three minutes. Every Christmas I call. Every Christmas my mother answers. Every Christmas we cry together for three minutes. Never any words."

She began to weep softly. But then a most radiant smile came to her face as she added, "It is something. It is enough." Through those bleak winter days, I remembered and was buoyed by her joy.

A few months later I sat before a bonfire at a rural retreat center during a service of welcome to Salvadoran refugees who had made it safely to the United States. A woman who had witnessed the murder of her husband and three sons sat beside me. She clapped as we sang a hymn of praise. Then she jumped up, the first to begin a dance around the bright flames shooting toward the sky. She encouraged others, grabbing hands and widening the circle until no one was left sitting on the logs.

Such joy can only be understood as welling up out of "the peace of God, which surpasses all understanding." We can find no rational explanation for this rich capacity for celebration in the midst of overwhelming grief. It is precisely when the world gives out, our own resources are depleted, and sorrow is all around that we are thrown back into the arms of God. There, we experience again the comforting embrace of a faithful God, who has shared our sorrows and taken up our burden. And that is cause for joy.

Jesus' analogy of birth is a beautiful one. A woman labors through waves of intense pain to bring a new life into the world. The agony of a moment (eternally long though it may seem) is overshadowed by the joy of a lifetime.

God restores the fortunes of Zion, brings the exiles home, causes rivers to flow where once there was desert. And the harvest is bountiful, brought home with accompanying shouts of joy.

Someone has said that "joy is the infallible sign of the presence of God." Where there is no joy, God is absent. Those words are an important reminder in difficult times.

Living as we do in a world that suffers so much, two opposing possibilities can easily tempt us: either to turn our backs and live oblivious to the pain or to allow the pain to overwhelm us and despair to take up residence in our hearts. The truly faithful option is to face the pain and live joyfully in the midst of it. Those who suffer most remind us of how tragic and arrogant it would be for us to lose hope on behalf of people who have not lost theirs. They are teachers of joy.

They are like John, long before he was known as the Baptist. While still in Elizabeth's womb, the baby John "leaped for joy" upon the greeting of Mary, the mother of Jesus (Luke 1:44). These two miraculously pregnant women—one old and believed barren, the other a young virgin—shared three months together, days of tremulous excitement over the quiet revolution that was about to be accomplished through them. Years later, when they had to endure the horrifying deaths of their sons, the memory of the joy of those early weeks and the promises of God's faithfulness likely carried them through.

Other teachers of joy are among us today. Dr. Janelle Goetcheus gave up a lucrative suburban medical practice to move with her family into Christ's House, a health-care facility for the homeless in inner-city Washington. Every day she cares for people who suffer from infections, foot problems, tuberculosis, pneumonia, and a variety of other illnesses related to exposure to the elements and poor nutrition.

Contrary to what one might expect, Dr. Goetcheus does not view her choice as a sacrifice. "I find that just being with them is a gift to my soul," she says of her patients at the house and in the city's shelters. "That doesn't mean I don't ache. My inner self just aches when I come out of a shelter....But what gives me the deepest joy is the sense that I'm trying to listen to God and be obedient to what God is asking."

Several years ago in North Carolina, Chrissy was born HIV-positive, and she spent much of her young life in hospitals. As a toddler, she loved to hear stories of Alice's adventures, both in Wonderland and through the looking glass. Chrissy particularly liked the idea of "un-birthdays." She exclaimed, "Everybody has a birthday, but we all can have 364 un-birthday parties a year!"

Chrissy managed to have at least one "un-birthday" every week, decorating her hospital room with balloons and asking visitors, "Would you like a piece of my un-birthday cake?" When she saw another patient in the hall struggling to get around with a severely fractured leg, she told him, "You need to have a party," and she arranged one. Chrissy died at the age of four, but she lived a life marked by joy, a legacy that she left to those who knew her.

Lindsay, a great-niece of my friend Mary Etta Perry, was almost four when she began gymnastics lessons. She became quite proficient at back bends, somersaults, and cartwheels. A few months later, she attended Vacation Bible School at her church. During "graduation" at the end of the session, each child had a line to recite. When Lindsay's turn came, she walked out on the stage, looked around at the crowd, and became frightened. The words would not come; she did a cartwheel.

As she took her seat next to her mother, to the cheers of the delighted audience of parents, Lindsay said quietly, "I forgot my line, but I remembered the cartwheel." I try to think of Lindsay as a role model. When she couldn't remember what came next, she leaped for joy anyway. May we all be so full of spontaneity and grace!

Contrary to what we often hear these days, life carries no guarantees of ease or comfort. The work of faith is hard. If we have committed ourselves to following Jesus, we will not escape the world's pain—because into the pain is where Jesus walked.

But like the infant John, when we are being faithful, we will instinctively leap and swirl and dance in the presence of God. Then will our "gloom be like the noonday." No darkness can overwhelm us. The light of Christ's presence will flood even the worst of days, inviting us back to celebration. Then the beautiful image of Isaiah 55:12-13 will be ours:

> For you shall go out in joy,
>   and be led back in peace;
> the mountains and the hills before you
>   shall burst into song,
>   and all the trees of the field
>   shall clap their hands.
>   Instead of the thorn
>   shall come up the cypress;

instead of the brier shall come up the myrtle;
and it shall be to the Lord for a memorial,
for an everlasting sign that shall not be cut off.

Amen.

FOR PRAYER AND DISCUSSION

1. In what ways does my life reflect the joy of Christ?

2. How have I experienced the truth of crucifixion with enough depth to understand the joy of resurrection?

3. How do I experience the "peace of God, which surpasses all understanding"?

Courage

Then Shall Your Light Rise

ILITARY EYES PEERED CONSTANTLY from the tower that rose above Duncan Village, an isolated black township in South Africa. At night, powerful floodlights aided the eyes, searching out "suspicious activity" in any corner. I arrived in the afternoon and, under the tower's watchful eye, was greeted by a young man active in the struggle against apartheid. It was April 1988, and South Africa was still very much in the grip of racial hatred.

We walked unhindered for almost an hour, with Jam-Jam telling me stories of the courage of his comrades in the face of police brutality and terror while I took pictures of the misery that greeted us. Jam-Jam himself had recently spent ten months in prison, where he was kept in a cold cell, fed cornmeal infested with worms, and tortured.

Soon an armored personnel carrier appeared on the horizon and moved slowly toward us. Eight members of the South African Defense Forces, waving rifles, surrounded us, ordering us to the military "strong point." Soldiers escorted us at gunpoint past the rows of barbed wire that surrounded the military headquarters and ushered us into an interrogation room to await an officer of the security police.

When he arrived, the officer spoke rapidly in Afrikaans to the other military personnel, then changed to brusque English as he faced us. He checked my passport, told me it was illegal under the current state of emergency to take pictures in a black area, and warned me against taking "unnecessary propaganda" about his country back home or "creating a rumble" among the people.

Then he turned to Jam-Jam, shaking his finger and threatening. He promised Jam-Jam that he would be back in detention if he didn't give up his "subversive activities." Jam-Jam's response was immediate. He reached into his back pocket and took out his small New Testament. Putting it in front of the officer's face, he said, "Sir, I am a Christian." A brief moment of silence descended as the arrogance of evil met the quiet power of the gospel.

SCRIPTURE

You are the light of the world. A city built on a hill cannot be hid. No one after lighting a lamp puts it under the bushel basket, but on the lampstand, and it gives light to all the house. In the same way, so let your light shine before others, so that they may see your good works and give glory to [God] in heaven.

→ Matthew 5:14-16

Finally, be strong in the Lord and in the strength of his power. Put on the whole armor of God, so that you may be able to stand against the wiles of the devil. For our struggle is not against enemies of blood and flesh, but against the rulers, against the authorities, against the cosmic powers of this present darkness, against the spiritual forces of evil in heavenly places. Therefore take up the whole armor of God, so that you may be able to withstand on that evil day, and having done everything, to stand firm.

Stand therefore, and fasten the belt of truth around your waist, and put on the breastplate of righteousness. As shoes

for your feet put on whatever will make you ready to proclaim the gospel of peace. With all of these, take the shield
of faith, with which you will be able to quench all the flam-
ing arrows of the evil one. Take the helmet of salvation, and
the sword of the Spirit, which is the word of God. Pray in
the Spirit at all times in every prayer and supplication.

↪ Ephesians 6:10-18

Therefore, my beloved,...work out your own salvation with
fear and trembling; for it is God who is at work in you,
enabling you both to will and to work for his good pleasure.
Do all things without murmuring and arguing, so that you
may be blameless and innocent, children of God without
blemish in the midst of a crooked and perverse generation,
in which you shine like stars in the world.

↪ Philippians 2:12-15

REFLECTION

Many years ago, I heard a Korean Christian talk about his experiences of imprisonment and torture at the hands of his government. His story could have come from Chile, Argentina, the
Philippines, El Salvador, Guatemala, Russia, Uganda, Liberia—
any place where Christians have faced persecution for their
faith. I am told that more Christians have been martyred in the
twentieth century than in the previous nineteen centuries com-
bined. One statement made by the Korean Christian has stayed
with me over the years: "In our country, courage is commonplace; in your country, what should be commonplace is called
courage."

We in the United States have been lulled too easily into taking belief for granted rather than living out of a vibrant, courageous faith. Our assessment of evil often comes down to narrow
definitions of personal immorality, rather than to an understanding of the entrenched evil in the world's systems and institutions.

We will not face the kind of persecution that the early believers encountered. The Book of Acts relates numerous accounts of the apostles' being dragged into courts, flogged, imprisoned, martyred. Being a Christian then required exceptional courage, a courage required in many parts of the world today. We in the United States may not have to face martyrdom, but the witness of scripture demands that we live each day as if our faith matters—and urges us to side with those of whom exceptional courage is required.

From across the globe come testimonies to the power of courage in the face of unspeakable evil. In the former Soviet Union, the Soviet secret police kept a close watch on citizens' activities. They chose to ignore an old woman who was badly crippled with multiple sclerosis; they discounted her on the basis of her appearance. What they didn't know was that every morning the woman's husband propped her in front of a typewriter. With her gnarled index finger, she painstakingly translated parts of the Bible and devotional books into the language of her people, a page or two a day. As she typed, she prayed for those who would read the words.

On the other side of the world, at two o'clock one morning, came a knock on the door where Victoria Diaz Carro lived. Her father, head of a union, was taken two decades ago by twenty-five members of the militia to the torture chambers of a Chilean prison and never heard from again. Victoria Diaz Carro and other relatives of the "disappeared" began creating *arpilleras*—"embroideries" of life and death—in response to their tragedy. With sorrow as warp, and hope as woof, these women began weaving the stories of their lives. Begun as a means of supporting their families, their colorful artwork took on spiritual significance as well, breaking down barriers of isolation and fear. Some of the *arpilleras* were confiscated, considered dangerous depictions of the political situation that prevailed in Chile then. These women disturbed the fabric of a country with cloth and thread.

In May 1992, at about four o'clock one afternoon, Serbian mortar fire killed twenty-two people standing in line outside a bakery in Sarajevo in the former Yugoslavia. For the next twenty-two days, Vedran Smailovic, a cellist in the Sarajevo symphony, brought a chair and his cello to that deserted spot at four o'clock. With Serbian shells crashing around him, he played Albinoni's *Adagio* to honor each of the martyrs.

Such stories may inspire us, but they also remind us that such courage is foreign in our day-to-day existence. No torturers wait for us in the night; no shells fall around us by day. Yet the world needs the courage of each of us.

Perhaps it's courage like that of my friend Arlene Kiely. Arlene worked at a children's hospital. A teacher asked her to help a child with some schoolwork. Arlene didn't realize until she got there that the student was on the burn unit, experiencing great pain and barely able to respond. She stumbled through the English lesson, ashamed at putting him through such a senseless exercise. The next morning a nurse asked her, "What did you do to that boy?" Before Arlene could finish apologizing, the nurse interrupted her: "You don't understand. His whole attitude has changed. It's as though he's decided to live." The boy explained later that he had completely given up hope until Arlene had arrived. With joyful tears, he said, "They wouldn't send somebody to work on nouns and verbs with a dying boy, would they?"

We are not terribly distant from days when upholding the dignity of all God's children brought severe persecution in this country. On September 15, 1963, at 10:22 A.M., a bomb exploded at Sixteenth Street Baptist Church in Birmingham, Alabama —the Ku Klux Klan's response to the desegregation of Birmingham's schools. Four schoolgirls died instantly. In that same city, fire hoses and vicious dogs were turned on marching children. Throughout the South, black men were lynched and Freedom Riders were beaten. Segregation seemed destined to stay.

Flora Smith, whose grandfather was a slave, was arrested at the age of fifty-six for praying on the steps of Birmingham's city hall during the height of the civil rights movement. The day before Mother's Day 1963, she woke up and told herself, "I'm going to go to jail today, and be somebody's mother tomorrow."

I met Flora thirty years later, when members of the Baptist Peace Fellowship of North America went to Sixteenth Street Baptist Church carrying their "Birmingham Confession." The document identified their denomination's failure to speak out against racism thirty years before as a "sin against the Holy Spirit." When the gathered congregation began singing "We Shall Overcome," Flora Smith was the first person on her feet. Arms crossed and hands clasped around the sanctuary. I asked her if in 1963 she ever thought that blacks and whites would be sitting in that church together singing freedom songs. Tears welled in her eyes as she replied, "Praise the good Lord, I never thought I'd see this day."

Fannie Lou Hamer, a prophet of the civil rights movement, led freedom marchers in singing "This Little Light of Mine" at every opportunity. The obstacles to change often felt overwhelming, but the movement was fueled by faith. Each and every soul involved in the freedom struggle took seriously the light entrusted to them as followers of Jesus. What seemed impossible was made real by the light of faith.

Much of our spirituality today pacifies us, invites us to escape to a gentle, unreal place far removed from the spiritual warfare about which the author of Ephesians writes: He warns of "cosmic powers" and "spiritual forces of evil"—rendered "principalities and powers" in other translations. To tackle these forces requires the "armor of God"—truth, righteousness, peace, faith, salvation—and, above all, prayer, our greatest weapon in this battle.

The Trappist monk Thomas Merton used to say that, like the great theologian Karl Barth, he prayed every day with his

Bible in one hand and the newspaper in the other. He saw his contemplative prayer as a means of engagement with the world, not an escape. To ignore the world's suffering is to deny the power of evil in the world. And to deny that power is to allow its victims to remain victims.

Through prayer, we claim the power of the Son of God over against the other powers. We celebrate the victory that he won over death—in all its forms. Through prayer, we empty ourselves of the world and find ourselves filled with the Spirit. We become partners with God the Creator on behalf of light and life and participants in the world's healing. Through prayer, we come to know our "spirit" as that spark of God within us that leads us on toward faith, truth, and courage.

Our Savior was audacious. He triumphed over sin! He rose from the dead! How can we be complacent? Many pathways of response lie before us but only one responsibility: to shine like lights, reflecting the truth of Christ.

All that we are called to as Christians—justice, compassion, and confession; surrender, simplicity, and gratitude; perseverance, solidarity, and reconciliation—all require courage. Our courage may be what the world most needs.

Several years ago, a Native American friend said, "If Christians actually lived the way the Bible calls them to, the world would be transformed today." I believe he's right. The Bible requires that we take our faith seriously and pray for the courage to follow the way of Jesus.

In South Africa I often asked people I met if they thought apartheid would end in their lifetime. "Not in my lifetime," was a common answer. "Probably not in mine or my children's," one older woman added, "but perhaps in their children's."

A ten year old in the township of Mamelodi, outside Pretoria, was more optimistic. He was sure that he would live to see an end to the system of racial segregation. When I asked if he thought his children would grow up without apartheid, he answered confidently, "I will see to it."

In South Africa, children lit candles in windows as signs of their resistance to apartheid. The South African security forces pushed into homes to blow them out. The children laughed and said, "They are afraid of candles." But the police knew that these were more than wax and flame: They were symbols of a promise and a hope. They were weapons of courage.

Ultimately, courage triumphed. Apartheid was overcome. And those young children are helping to build the new South Africa. This truth sustains them: "The light shines in the darkness, and the darkness did not overcome it" (John 1:5).

That is our hope and promise as well. Jesus came into the world as light to brighten every dark corner. To follow him means to reflect his truth. The world waits. Shine like a light!

FOR PRAYER AND DISCUSSION

1. What would it mean for me to live courageously?

2. How can my prayer life connect me to the courage of others who are being persecuted?

3. In what ways do I "shine like a light" and reflect the truth of Christ?

About the Author

JOYCE HOLLYDAY is a peace activist and journalist. Her work has encompassed retreat leadership, hospital chaplaincy, and advocacy. Her ministry has crossed many national and international borders, including South Africa, Zaire, Norway, and Australia. She was a founding member of "Witness for Peace in Nicaragua," a nonviolent national effort that maintained an ongoing presence of North Americans in Nicaragua's war zones.

Having served as associate editor of *Sojourners* magazine for fifteen years, Hollyday is now a columnist and contributing editor for the magazine. Currently she is a Woodruff Scholar at Candler School of Theology, Emory University. A writer of numerous articles and books, her most recent book is *Clothed with the Sun: Biblical Women, Social Justice, and Us*.